WHAT TO DO WHEN EXPECTING

WEEK BY WEEK GUIDE OF YOUR PREGNANCY JOURNEY

D'LOVE THERAPIST

Table of Contents

INTRODUCTION

Weekly pregnancy schedule

Are you anticipating your first pregnancy ultrasound or your first time feeling your baby kick? Consider this pregnancy schedule for the next nine months to be your comprehensive road map.

Your body is adjusting to your baby's daily changes while you are pregnant. With each week, month, and trimester of your pregnancy coming with new changes and milestones for both you and your unborn child, this pregnancy tracker will help you better understand them.

Continue reading to find out more about what to anticipate happening each week of your pregnancy, including how big your baby is each week.

common early pregnancy symptoms that you might encounter, ways to get ready for labor once you've reached the third trimester, and indications that labor is about to start. With this manual, you'll comprehend what's happening and why, both internally and externally.

WEEK 1 AND 2

EXPLORE PREGNANCY WEEK 1 AND 2

Your body starts preparing for ovulation and fertilization in weeks 1 and 2 of pregnancy, which take place in week 3.

preparations for ovulation

No baby or embryo is visible, unfortunately. Not yet, at least. All that is present are an anxious egg and a large number of eager sperm at each race's starting line.

However, during weeks 1 and 2 of pregnancy—the week before and right after your last menstrual period—your body is hard at work preparing for the big O, or ovulation, which is the event that gives birth to the baby.

Your uterus is currently getting ready for the arrival of a fertilized egg, though you won't be able to tell for sure if the egg and sperm were a good match until next week.

Unexpectedly, during the first week of pregnancy, you are not actually pregnant! The first day of your most recent period is used to determine your due date.

Be a good landlord while your uterus is getting ready for its new occupant. Consider the next two weeks as a final check-up before the baby takes the reins. Although you are not yet officially pregnant, it is not too early to act as though you are. Start taking your prenatal vitamin, quit smoking and drinking, and adopt a prenatal-friendly diet and exercise regimen.

Reduce the heat to increase fertility.

Trying to conceive a child? Disconnect from the electric blanket and keep each other warm the traditional way. Studies have shown that prolonged, excessive heat, such as that produced by heating pads, electric blankets, heated seats, and even laptops placed on a man's lap, can negatively affect those temperamental testes by slowing sperm production (and you want sperm in abundance right now!). Additionally, the amount of cuddling you'll need to do to stay warm will produce heat that can actually result in pregnancy.

Additional strategies to improve your chances of finding a fertilized egg: Try to avoid oral sex before the main event since saliva can affect sperm activity and motility negatively. and you want them to be fully functional.

Symptoms of Pregnancy Weeks 1 and 2

Your temperature drops then rises.

Increased Cervical Mucus: This Week's Tips

eat plenty of folic acid

Undoubtedly, when you're expecting, your body works extra hard. To help it get the extra nutrients it needs to grow a baby, get 400 to 600 micrograms of folic acid daily from all sources, including your prenatal vitamin and foods high in folate.

According to research, taking folic acid daily from the time you start trying to conceive until after the baby is born has significant advantages for both the mother and the child's health.

Folic acid (and its natural form, folate) has been shown to lower your risk of gestational diabetes, preterm labor, and miscarriage. It can also help lower the risk of birth defects like congenital heart and neural tube defects in your baby.

WEEK 3

EXPLORE WEEK 3 PREGNANCY

Congratulations! Although it will be a few weeks before you can confirm the news with a pregnancy test, you have officially conceived and are in your first month of pregnancy at 3 weeks pregnant.

The tiny group of cells that will eventually give birth to your child are growing quickly this week. One of the earliest indicators of pregnancy, a heightened sense of smell, may be brought on by rising hormone levels.

There is an embryo here! Your developing fetus is still just a collection of developing cells. It resembles a pinhead in size.

Implantation

For the time being, it will appear as though nothing is happening on the outside, but this will only last for a few weeks. Your body is preparing to receive the blastocyst (which will soon become your baby!) that is traveling to the uterus, where it will spend the next nine months if your timing is right and you had sex during ovulation. If this is the case, your egg has been fertilized by one fortunate sperm.

Week 3 of Pregnancy Symptoms

Reduced abdominal tension

This Week's Tips for You on Metallic Taste

Add more iron and vitamin C.

Add berries to your breakfast cereal.

Iron is absorbed more readily by your body when it is combined with foods high in vitamin C; iron is a nutrient you need to support your increased blood volume.

Vitamin C can be found in kiwis, mangoes, strawberries, melons, bell peppers, tomatoes, asparagus, and other fruits and vegetables. Soy products, beef, poultry, and dried fruit all contain iron.

Put off coloring your hair.

Experts concur that it is better to be safe than sorry when it comes to hair coloring. So postpone getting a touch-up until your second trimester, or after week 14 of pregnancy.

Stick to highlights rather than root lightening or root-to-tip color changes when you return to the salon (the chemicals won't touch your scalp this way) and ask for a gentler coloring option.

Additionally, keep in mind that even with your regular formula, hormonal changes can cause your hair to react differently. As a result, you might not get the results you were hoping for. Consider trying a test strand before you do your entire head to be sure.

When dining out, try to choose healthy options.

When ordering takeout or dining out, finding healthy options is simpler than you might imagine. Eat grilled fish, chicken, veal, or lean beef entrees with gorgeous greens if you're craving Italian food. Also recommended are cheese, seafood that is safe for pregnant women, and pasta and pizza with fresh tomato sauce.

Select foods high in calcium.

Calcium is important for the health of your heart, nerves, and muscles in addition to helping you and your unborn child develop and maintain strong, healthy bones. Your unborn child will take calcium from your bones if you don't get enough of it while you're pregnant.

Consume four daily servings (1,000 milligrams) of foods like hard or pasteurized cheese, frozen or Greek yogurt, calcium-fortified juice, or cereal.

When you feel sick, replenish your fluids.

You might have a stomach bug or food poisoning rather than morning sickness if it is accompanied by cramps, fever, or diarrhea.

However, the treatment is the same whether your stomach is churning due to hormones, a virus, or that egg salad you had for lunch: Stay hydrated and get plenty of rest, especially if you're losing fluids due to vomiting or diarrhea.

Drink plenty of water, diluted juice (white grape is the gentlest on the stomach), clear broth, weak decaf tea, or hot water with lemon to help with gas. Suck on Popsicles if you find it difficult to take a sip.

Consume a lot of protein

Eat three servings of protein each day to encourage the growth of new tissue for your unborn child. The recommended serving size for meat, such as skinless chicken or lean beef, is 3 ounces, or about the same as a deck of cards. Eggs, fish, dairy products, and legumes are additional excellent sources of protein

WEEK 4

EXPLORE PREGNANCY WEEK 4

Your body is starting to form the placenta and amniotic sac in week 4 of pregnancy.

This week, you may experience symptoms like abdominal discomfort and tender breasts. As the group of cells that will eventually become your baby penetrates the lining of your uterus, you may also experience implantation bleeding. (However, if you haven't yet noticed any symptoms, that is also completely normal.)

Still no symptoms?

Most likely, you're unaware of all the commotion. Early pregnancy symptoms like mood swings, bloating, and cramping can be bothersome for some women, while others don't even register them.

It might be too early to see a reliable result on your pregnancy test, regardless of how you're feeling or not feeling.

This week, the blastocyst that will eventually become your child is starting to attach itself to the uterine lining through a process known as implantation.

As that bundle of cells penetrates the uterine wall, implantation bleeding can happen up to 25% of the time. Your expected period usually starts earlier than the implantation bleeding, which is typically very scant and either light pink, light red, or light brown in color.

The bleeding is not a sign that something is wrong, so don't worry about mistaking it for your period or worry about it.

It's possible that you will feel some pressure in your abdomen, but don't be alarmed! additionally, your breasts might feel a little tender and enlarge (but brace yourself for more growth spurts!).

Week 4 of pregnancy symptoms

PMS-like symptoms from implant bleeding

Advice for This Week

Remember to take vitamin D.

Your body gets the majority of its vitamin D from the sun or fortified milk. You'll need to get your D from other sources if you don't drink the white stuff.

That's because vitamin D aids in calcium absorption and is crucial for maintaining strong teeth and bones.

Numerous prenatal vitamins contain vitamin D, which is also present in fortified milk, orange juice, and egg yolks. Consult your physician about how much you require (600 IU is the standard recommendation among the expectant set, but some may need 1,000 IU or more).

Good fats include healthy fats.

Your baby requires fat, particularly necessary fats like omega-3 fatty acids. One of those omega-3s, DHA, is crucial for your baby's developing brain and eyes because it is a crucial part of the human brain and retina.

Fish that are safe for pregnancy, like trout and wild salmon, as well as DHA-fortified eggs, are good sources of DHA. DHA is also present in prenatal vitamins and supplements, including vegetarian ones, if you can't stand fish.

Don't smoke around others.

Even if you don't smoke, the baby could still be at risk if those close to you do. The risk of miscarriage, low birth weight, ectopic pregnancy, and other complications may rise if you are exposed to secondhand smoke, according to recent research. So, make every effort to avoid it.

Try a different comfort food.

Frequently, a food that at first seems to be a comfort food (i.e., one of the few things you can stomach) later develops a negative connotation and, because you've consumed so much of it, begins to cause nausea again.

For instance, substitute another comforting carb if you're sick to death of saltine crackers and they're starting to make you queasy.

Schedule a pregnancy appointment.

Now is the perfect time to schedule your first medical appointment, if you haven't already. Since early prenatal care is so crucial, it's best to schedule an appointment as soon as you have a positive pregnancy test. Some OB/GYNs request that you wait until you are at least 6 to 8 weeks pregnant before a visit.

Make sure to first do your homework on the type of doctor or midwife you really want.

Prevent foodborne illness

Even though you may only be eating for one and a half people these days, your menu just got a lot smaller. Why should we avoid sushi, runny eggs, and uncooked cookie dough? to prevent diseases like listeria and salmonella that are transmitted through food.

Undercooked proteins like poultry, eggs, meat, or fish, as well as unpasteurized dairy products and juices, are some of the most frequent causes of food poisoning.

In the unlikely event that salmonella causes food poisoning, the bug will most likely have to run its (unpleasant) course. It's unlikely that your baby will be in any danger, so don't worry.

WEEK 5

EXPLORE WEEK 5 PREGNANCY

You are currently in your second trimester at 5 weeks pregnant. Your hCG hormone levels are high enough to produce a positive pregnancy test result this week, and you may already be experiencing early symptoms like fatigue and nausea.

And your infant? Your unborn child's heart and circulatory system are growing, and the embryo is starting to resemble a fetus.

The neural tube, which will eventually develop into your baby's brain and spinal cord, is another organ that will develop this week. But that open-door policy will end by the following week.

Early signs of pregnancy

There will also be other early pregnancy indicators. Similar to the feeling of exhaustion that may have swept over you. Also those delicate breasts. Or perhaps you experienced a brief attack of nausea after smelling a dish you usually don't find offensive.

The onset of pregnancy hormones

This week, large amounts of hormones—chemical signals that travel throughout your body and combine to bring about physical changes—are being produced in large quantities.

Furthermore, don't be shocked if you occasionally feel as though these hormones are controlling your life.

Week 5 of Pregnancy Symptoms

Food aversions and cravings

Fatigue\sNausea

this week's suggestions for excessive saliva

Avoid using the toilet.

Score! Throughout your pregnancy, you are exempt from litter-box duty. This is because cat feces may contain a parasite that can cause toxoplasmosis, a disease that is harmful to unborn children.

Additionally, you shouldn't play in or clean out a child's sandbox because neighborhood outdoor cats might use it as a litter box. You also shouldn't eat raw or undercooked meat or feed it to your cat. Request assistance from your spouse, a friend, or a family member.

However, unless the risk of forgoing a dental X-ray outweighs the relatively low risk of radiation exposure to the baby, it is advised to postpone getting one until after the baby is born.

If you do get an X-ray, cover your lower belly with an abdominal shield or lead apron.

Know the foods you should avoid.

It's time to remove some foods from the menu, including raw sprouts, mercury-filled or unpasteurized fish, unpasteurized dairy products and juices, undercooked meat, and eggs (they can cause foodborne illnesses that can be bad for baby).

Hot dogs and deli meats should also be avoided because they may contain nitrates and nitrites. In addition, you should reduce your caffeine intake and, if you haven't already, give up alcohol.

soothe a stomach ache

Do you need to calm your stomach? Consider munching on a snack that is high in protein and complex carbohydrates, such as granola and yogurt or whole wheat crackers and cheese. Alternately, omit the solids and savor a smoothie or soup.

Make sure to consume eight to ten glasses of fluids daily, especially if vomiting is causing you to become dehydrated. Ginger may also be helpful for your ailments. Cook with it, such as in ginger-carrot soup or ginger muffins, brew tea with it, munch on ginger biscuits, eat crystallized ginger, or indulge in ginger candies.

Ask your doctor about taking a vitamin B6 supplement or switching your prenatal vitamin from one loaded with iron to one higher in B6.

Find out how to control bloat

Some of the healthiest foods can make you feel bloated; it's like a cosmic joke.

and certainly not in the mood to consume your vegetables. Additionally, due to pregnancy hormones, gas and bloating are common during pregnancy.

Choose healthy alternatives that won't cause you to feel bloated, such as strawberries or mangoes in place of broccoli.

Eat poached chicken breast instead of those formerly adored chicken fingers, and munch on bagel chips instead of potato chips.

Another easy method for reducing pregnancy belly bubbles is to drink plain water rather than sparkling water.

Does morning sickness exercise help?

Exercise during the first trimester is debatable, especially if you're experiencing morning sickness. That all depends on how you feel after working out.

When you are five weeks pregnant and feeling queasy, go outside for a quick walk. After about 15 minutes, you'll probably feel better thanks to the exercise and the fresh air.

Choose your proteins.

You've had a falling out with meat (and chicken, and fish...) and now you can't even be in the same room together, let alone share a plate, despite the fact that you know you need your protein.

In the meantime, get your protein from cottage cheese, yogurt, beans, or soy products, particularly tofu or edamame. Eventually, you'll be able to stomach these meaty foods once more. Or think about quinoa, a nutty grain with a powerful protein punch in a warm package.

Brighten up your diet with yellow vegetables (which are frequently easier to take), like carrots or yams, if leafy greens turn you a not-so-delicate shade of chartreuse. alternatively, try the beta-carotene found in cantaloupe, mangoes, peaches, and apricots

WEEK 6

EXPLORE WEEK 6 0f PREGNANCY

This week, your baby is beginning to resemble a baby more and more; the little one's head is developing, and the cheeks, chin, and jaws are also starting to form.

Due to symptoms like heartburn, nausea, and frequent urination in week 6 of pregnancy, you may also feel fully pregnant.

Smile!

This week, the cheeks chin, and jaws of your child's face are starting to form.

Often urinating

Even though the outside of your body may not yet show signs of pregnancy, every time you feel sick, bloated, or devour your sixth grapefruit of the day—which is funny because you've never craved grapefruit before—you'll be reminded that you're six weeks pregnant.

another hints? More often than not, you are in the restroom. One of the most typical symptoms of pregnancy, especially early on, frequent urination is a symptom no pregnant woman enjoys, especially when it interferes with the sleep you really need right now.

Why? One effect of the pregnancy hormone hCG is an increase in blood flow to your pelvic region, which is beneficial for greater sexual pleasure but problematic when you are an hour into a two-hour movie at the theater.

Additionally, your kidneys are getting better at removing waste from your body.

You've got a perfect (pee) storm on your hands when you consider that your expanding uterus is starting to press down on your bladder, leaving less space for urine storage. Fortunately, once the uterus rises into the abdominal cavity in the second trimester, this pressure frequently subsides.

Observational advice: To guarantee that your bladder is completely empty each time you urinate, lean forward. Once you believe you are finished, urinate once more. You might make fewer trips to the restroom if you do it this way. However, resist the urge to reduce your fluid intake because your body requires a constant flow of liquids.

Acid reflux and indigestion

The bad news is that there is almost no chance that you will be heartburn-free for the ensuing nine months.

That's because the muscle band that typically keeps digestive juices from backing up at the top of the stomach relaxes.

The good news is that by avoiding foods like citrus fruits and tomatoes — yes, that includes pizza and pasta sauce as well as greasy and spicy foods, rushing through meals, and belly-cinching clothing — you can lessen the symptoms. Additionally, it's a good idea to finish eating dinner at least four hours prior to going to bed and to sleep with your head elevated on a pillow.

Week 6 Pregnancy Symptoms

breast sensitivity and modifications

Fatigue

nausea and diarrhoea

This Week's Tips for You on Bloating and Gas

Avoid avoiding all seafood

Not all fish are created equal for the pregnant population. Don't avoid all healthy seafood, though you should avoid high-mercury fish like tilefish from the Gulf of Mexico, shark, swordfish, orange roughy, bigeye tuna, marlin, and king mackerel.

Try to consume two to three servings of well-cooked shellfish, canned light tuna, salmon (wild-caught is best), or cod per week as fish is one of the best sources of DHA (a healthy omega-3 fatty acid).

Watch out for signs of UTI

You might have a urinary tract infection if it hurts to urinate or if you need to go but nothing comes (UTI). To be certain, consult your doctor.

A baby-safe antibiotic will probably be prescribed if you do have a UTI. After week 6 of pregnancy, your risk of contracting this infection increases.

Stay bland

Do not worry if seeing a saltine makes you want to scream. Contrary to popular belief, you have more options.

The key words here are still dry and bland, but that term applies to more than just a cracker. You can stash dry cereal, pretzels, rice cakes, bread that has been well-toasted, bread sticks, and pretzels in your purse or keep them on your nightstand.

Take some steps.

Making the decision to exercise is one thing; finding the time to do it is another, especially if you frequently feel queasy.

Instead of waiting until you find a half-hour to work out, the best approach is to schedule a specific time in your day for it (hint: You never will).

Pick nutritious treats.

Every sweet or salty junk food you are currently craving has a healthier alternative that, when combined with some willpower, can satisfy both your taste buds and your baby.

Replace greasy chips with baked or soy alternatives. You could also eat some rice cakes, pretzels, or air-popped popcorn (tossed with some Parmesan for that salty kick you crave).

Instead of that king-sized Snickers bar, indulge your inner chocoholic with a cup of hot chocolate or a single-serving Fudgsicle.

Do you want ice cream so bad? Instead, opt for frozen yogurt, and add fresh berries to yours to boost its nutritional value.

Treat yourself

It's completely safe to paint your nails, so relax. Profit from this now, as pregnancy hormones may cause them to become bigger and stronger than ever.

Although there is no evidence that the chemicals in acrylics are harmful to you or your fetus, you might want to wait to follow these suggestions until your baby is born just to be safe.

It might also be a good idea to use non-toxic, water-based polish ingredients, and a well-ventilated salon is also recommended (this is true whether or not you are pregnant).

Try a clear nail hardener and reapply frequently if you notice that your nails have grown weak or brittle because your hormones didn't get the memo (and make sure you're getting enough calcium, too).

Get ready for your first prenatal appointment.

Although your home pregnancy test confirmed your pregnancy, it doesn't hurt to have a doctor confirm it. For this reason, you're likely looking forward to your first prenatal doctor's appointment. Expect this examination to be exciting and drawn out.

Prior to your appointment, find out from your doctor if there are any COVID-19 guidelines you need to be aware of and follow.

Upon arrival, you will undergo a thorough physical examination that includes a pelvic exam, Pap smear, and initial blood tests to identify your blood type, Rh factor, level of iron deficiency, and potential chromosomal abnormalities in your unborn child.

Additionally, you'll undergo tests for STIs, rubella immunity (German measles immunity), and genetic disorders that are specific to a particular ethnic group. Additionally, you'll have to pee into a cup so that your urine can be examined for bacteria, red and white blood cells, glucose, and protein.

Be prepared to provide lengthy answers to many questions regarding your health history? Can having sex harm your unborn child? Ask rather than just stand there!

Nothing is silly anymore, so keep that in mind. While you're at it, ask your doctor if you ought to undergo noninvasive prenatal testing (NIPT), a chromosomal abnormality screening that may be given as early as week 10 of pregnancy and is advised for some at-risk mothers.

Fun fact: Your embryo is 10,000 times larger than it was when it first entered your uterus at 7 weeks of pregnancy! Your baby is developing 100 new brain cells every minute while also growing quickly.

Morning sickness, tender breasts, and food intolerances are all common symptoms as you enter the second half of the first trimester.

WEEK 7

EXPLORE WEEK 7 0f PREGNANCY

Brain cells regenerate quickly.

As new brain cells are created at a rate of 100 per minute at 7 weeks pregnant, the majority of that growth is concentrated in the head (the better to store all those smarts). What do you call a young genius?

Know the symptoms

Your breasts are swollen

Your breasts are also getting fattier and the blood flow there is getting stronger. Your nipples might be a little more protruding than usual, but they are so delicate and sensitive that touching them might hurt.

The dark area around the nipple known as the areola has already grown darker and larger, and will continue to do so over the coming months.

Additionally, you'll see small, goose-bump-like spots on the areola. Montgomery's tubercles, which are these lumps, are sebaceous glands that lubricate the areola.

And if you're wondering why all of these changes are happening, this is the explanation: All of them are necessary to the crucial task of nursing your newborn in about 33 weeks!

Managing dietary aversions

You're not alone if the sight of a chicken breast these days makes you want to run out the door, or if the smell of Swiss cheese makes your stomach howl in agony. Food aversions during pregnancy are not only very common, but they can also be very perplexing, especially when a once-loved food suddenly makes you feel sick to your stomach and cold.

The best piece of advice is to cater to your new preferences. Keep your meals bland and uninteresting. If you can't stand the sight or smell of meat, consider substituting quinoa for protein. And be happy if your aversions are to foods you should be avoiding anyway.

7th week of pregnancy symptoms

often urinating

breast sensitivity and modifications

Fatigue

Food aversions and cravings

Acid reflux and indigestion

this week's suggestions for excessive saliva

Typically, cramping is normal.

If you get cramps in your stomach while you're expecting, it's probably nothing to worry about. Cramping is common in the first trimester, but if it is accompanied by shoulder or neck pain, contractions, wooziness, or discharge, call the doctor.

Fruit can be a friend.

Nature's sweetest bounty not only includes beneficial nutrients for both you and your unborn child, but fruit also plays a major role in maintaining your regularity.

Be aware of your workout sins

Here is a quick list of some exercises you should avoid while pregnant:

• Once the first trimester is over, avoid doing any back exercises.

• When exercising, try not to hold your breath.

• Avoid jerky or twisting motions because they might aggravate your joints' existing stress.

• Be cautious when performing any movements that could endanger your abdomen or test your sense of balance.

Exercise will soon become less oxygen-efficient for you, so stop when you're exhausted and stay cool.

safely treat skin conditions

Thanks to hormones, pregnancy can result in some pretty bizarre complexion complications, including melasma, a patchy skin discoloration, excessive oiliness or dryness (or both at once), acne, and blotchiness.

Washing your face two to three times a day with a thorough but gentle cleanser will help if pimples are the issue; harsh cleansers will only make skin more prone to irritation.

Additionally, gently exfoliate once a week, and then moisturize with a product that doesn't contain any oils. Skin that has been overly stripped is more prone to breakouts.

Indulge in wholesome cravings

What actions should you take when cravings occur? Depends, really. If you're fortunate enough to be craving fruits or vegetables, give in.

But if your cravings are pushing you to reach for a bowl of sugar-frosted cereal or a bag of kettle-cooked potato chips, try to fight them. Eat soy crisps, which are high in protein, or top your Cheerios with fresh fruit and a drizzle of honey.

If you're craving something you shouldn't be eating while you're expecting, such as unpasteurized soft cheese or sashimi, substitute something that tastes as much like the thing you're craving as possible, such as pasteurized feta and teriyaki salmon.

Contact your practitioner if you start to crave things like clay, ashes, or laundry starch that aren't foods. Such cravings might be a sign of a condition called pica, which is brought on by a nutrient shortage.

Provide for your dislikes

You're not the only one who finds the idea of eating a chicken breast nauseating. Pregnancy phobias are very prevalent.

Simply follow what works. Rejoice if your aversions are to foods that you should be avoiding anyway (sushi aversion, anyone?), keep your choices bland and boring, find substitutes for foods you can no longer stomach (think fruit if you can't stand the sight of veggies), and keep your diet bland and boring.

WEEK 8

EXPLORE WEEK 8 0f PREGNANCY

If you're one of the 75% of women who experience morning sickness, your clothes may be getting a little tight, even though you're probably not yet showing, and you may definitely feel pregnant.

Your baby is growing at a millimeter per day at this point in the pregnancy, and the lips, nose, and eyelids are starting to form.

Your infant is developing at an astounding rate. How has she performed so far this week? Your child is currently between the size of a blueberry and a raspberry, measuring between half and three quarters of an inch.

Daytime sickness

Yes, morning sickness—though the name can be deceiving—is that infamous rite of passage that comes with being pregnant. If you are one of the estimated 75% of pregnant women who experience morning sickness, you are all too aware that while it may begin in the morning, It can last all day and all night.

Nobody can say for sure what exactly makes them feel queasy, and does it really matter when they're about to throw away their cookies for the third time today?

though there are many theories. It might be caused by your body's increased levels of hCG and estrogen, the relaxation of the digestive tract muscles brought on by rising progesterone levels, or the rapid stretching of the uterine muscles, all of which would reduce the efficiency of digestion.

Whatever the reason, have courage; your baby is fine, even as you are cuddling the bowl. Try to eat frequently but only a small amount at a time. This will help your body fight pregnancy heartburn, which is another obstinate problem that will soon affect you.

Ask your doctor if you should take a pregnancy anti-nausea medication if you're really having morning sickness, such as if you've lost at least 5 pounds or can't keep anything down for more than eight hours.

fruit consumption during pregnancy

Fruit is always your friend, but while you're expecting, treat it like your best friend. Nature's sweetest bounty not only contains important vitamins and nutrients that are good for you and your baby, but it also plays a major role in maintaining your regularity — pass the prunes, please!

Your growing belly might also cause new pains above your neck. Your blood volume will rise by just under 50%, and combined with the pregnancy hormones, this may make you more prone to headaches.

Create a baby registry (or two)

It's not too early to consider the items you'll need to buy before the baby is born.

Put on some SPF.

Damn it, get out of here! Pregnancy-related hormonal fluctuations in many women can result in melasma, or dark spots on the skin and face.

As a result, your skin, freckles, and moles may appear darker, and your abdomen likely has a dark line running down the middle of it (the linea nigra). Your areolas might also be a darker shade.

You're not alone; between 50 and 75 percent of expectant mothers experience this condition. However, by wearing a wide-brimmed hat and sunscreen with an SPF of 30 or higher when you're outside, you may be able to stop melasma from getting worse.

Monitor your weight.

Throughout your 40 weeks of pregnancy, it's beneficial to gain weight gradually, but that doesn't mean you'll do so uniformly.

You might only put on two to four pounds during your first trimester, and if you have morning sickness, you might not put on any weight at all.

Start exercising slowly.

Start slowly if it's been a while since your last workout. Overdoing it increases your likelihood of quitting when you're just getting started and can result in injury, nausea, overheating, and plain old exhaustion.

Start out slowly when you exercise. Start with a 10-minute gentle warm-up, followed by 10-minutes of moderate exercise, and 10-minute cool-down. then weekly add five minutes to the moderate segment.

Eat smaller meals.

Being pregnant is never easy, but it can be particularly difficult when you want to start feeding yourself and your unborn child well.

Eat at least six smaller but nutrient-dense mini-meals and snacks throughout the day if large meals are a major turnoff for you.

In addition to being simpler for your queasy stomach to stomach, keeping your stomach slightly full is the best way to prevent it from emptying out.

Focus on less offensive foods right now, even if that means eating nothing but crackers.

Select wholesome crabs.

Has "crab" evolved into a four-letter word in your diet? Choose wholesome complex carbohydrates that will nourish your baby and meet your energy needs to redefine it.

The following list of nutritious carbohydrate choices reads like the line-up of a nutritional all-star team: Fresh fruits, dried and freeze-dried fruits, fresh vegetables, whole-grain breads, crackers, and cereals, baked potatoes (with the skin on), beans, and peas are all examples of food that can be consumed.

WEEK 9

EXPLORE WEEK 9 0f PREGNANCY

Tiny muscles began to form this week, but you won't be able to feel those tiny punches for at least another month or two.

Your child is currently about 1 inch long and the size of a medium green olive at 9 weeks pregnant, but no martinis, please.

On ultrasound, fetal cardiac activity can be heard.

However, it's not too early to hear something even though it's way too early to feel anything. Your baby's heart is large enough and sufficiently developed for a Doppler, a portable ultrasound device, to pick up cardiac activity.

If your doctor can't hear the sound yet, don't worry. It simply means that your shy guy is trying to hide in the recess of your uterus or is facing outward, making it difficult for the Doppler to locate the target.

You'll be able to hear that miraculous sound for yourself in a few weeks or during your next visit.

Being so exhausted!

At nine weeks pregnant, you might feel like you've had enough of the pregnancy symptoms: You're busting out on top, your clothes are getting tighter around the waist, and you're still running to the bathroom 100 times a day, usually to urinate.

You struggle to get out of bed in the morning, drag your feet all day, and are eager to get into bed as soon as you get home at night.

Sounds recognizable? Extreme fatigue during pregnancy is a typical symptom, particularly in the first trimester. And with good reason—having a child requires a lot of work. Your body is working extra hard to get ready for motherhood as the placenta, which is your unborn child's lifeline, develops.

Additionally, your body's metabolism and hormone levels have significantly increased, which causes blood sugar and blood pressure to drop, which is a recipe for fatigue. Use these recommendations to safely combat fatigue while pregnant.

Eating healthy

Instead of eating three large meals a day, concentrate on eating six small meals or snacks. And choose your snacks carefully to meet your baby's and your own nutritional needs without upsetting your uneasy stomach.

pregnancy symptoms

Often urinating

Fatigue

breast sensitivity and modifications

Acid reflux and indigestion

Gas and bloating

Tips for This Week's Constipation

Reduce heartburn

Are you experiencing heartburn, specifically? Heartburn, which often appears around the second month of pregnancy, is among the first signs of pregnancy for many women.

If staying away from greasy and spicy foods isn't working, consider taking antacids. They have more calcium, which you need anyway while pregnant.

Position

If lying on your stomach while you sleep is your preferred position, that's fine—at least, until your stomach reaches watermelon size, at which point you'll need to switch positions for obvious reasons.

It's best for you and your unborn child to sleep on your side during the second and third trimesters.

In addition to improving kidney function, this position relieves pressure on the vena cava, allowing for maximum blood flow and nutrition to the placenta.

eat plenty of fiber

Roughage, or foods high in fiber, will assist you in getting rid of waste. Consume whole grains, fruits and vegetables, beans and peas, whether fresh or dried.

You can also benefit from going green, and you don't just have to eat vegetables: On the other hand, make sure to limit those traditional cloggers: White bread, white rice, refined cereals, and pasta are examples of refined Increase the usefulness of your clothing

Every pregnant woman experiences that stage of fashion limbo sooner or later. You are currently too small for maternity clothing but too big for your jeans.

So, be imaginative. Buy a belly band to cover your unbuttoned pants and enhance your silhouette, or thread a rubber band around your jeans button, through the buttonhole, and back around the button.

Alternately, leave the back of your skirt unzipped and cover it with a blouse, sweater, or jacket to conceal the evidence.

That way, you can use your favorites for a few extra weeks. Grains

. Be smart about your wardrobe when you're ready to explore the world of maternity fashion. Buy as you expand, look outside the maternity section for adorable clothing that fits, and maintain your sense of fashion!

Stop being constipated

One pregnancy symptom that no one wants to discuss is constipation.

Looking for advice to get things going? Examine your supplements carefully first. Contrary to popular belief, many supplements that are beneficial to a pregnant body (such as prenatal vitamins, calcium, and iron supplements) can also cause constipation.

Speak with your doctor about possible substitutes like a slow-release supplement, an iron-free prenatal, or a vitamin with a stool softener. Additionally, you can improve your situation by including some form of exercise (a brisk walk, yoga)

And remember to go when you have to. as soon as is practical. Your bowel muscles may become weaker if you hold it in, making it more difficult to push out the poop. Also, keep in mind to postpone taking any medications, including herbal ones, until you have spoken with your doctor.

Employ cold compresses.

Pregnant women frequently experience breast tenderness, with symptoms ranging from a dull ache to a fullness sensation and sharp, shooting pains.

But there's a purpose behind all of this activity: Your body is increasing the blood flow to the area and storing fat, which will help prepare you for breastfeeding once the baby is born.

Apply an ice pack wrapped in a towel to your breasts until the pain goes away, which is typically in the second or third trimester. Alternately, if you'd rather be warm, take a warm shower.

WEEK 10

EXPLORE WEEK 10 0f PREGNANCY

As of this third month of your pregnancy, your unborn child has transitioned from an embryo to a fetus. At 10 weeks pregnant, you might only be beginning to show (though it's also normal if there aren't any symptoms of a bump yet), and you might also notice visible veins and increased vaginal discharge.

having spent so much time in the water.

Your baby is now truly resembling a human. Small indentations on the legs are developing into knees and ankles as bones and cartilage are developing. How magical is it that the arms can already flex, down to the elbows?

However, hold off on purchasing a baseball bat just yet. Even though your baby's arms are developing and growing stronger, they are all still incredibly small.

Symptoms could linger

Some of those amusing pregnancy symptoms might still be present. Totally clogged? Many expectant mothers experience constipation as a result of the large bowel's smooth muscles becoming sluggish due to those annoying pregnancy hormones.

Whole grains, fruits, and vegetables that contain fiber, as well as drinking lots of water and engaging in regular exercise, can all be beneficial.

Continue to experience nausea and vomiting? One or more of these morning sickness treatments may be advised by your doctor.

observable veins

You might also notice all the blue lines that have suddenly started crossing your breasts and abdomen on your skin.

Both people with light and dark complexions may have these visible veins. What you are seeing is an enlarged network of veins that is supplying more blood to your developing fetus.

You'll also notice that as your pregnancy goes on, the veins in your hands and feet appear bigger and more noticeable. The veins must maintain their volume in order to keep up with the average woman's 50 percent increase in blood volume during pregnancy.

Therefore, think of those blue lines as a badge of pregnancy: Wear them with pride and the assurance that once your baby is born and you are no longer breastfeeding, they will vanish forever (if you do).

constipation treatment

Constipation is a first trimester pregnancy symptom that is all-too-common. What can you do in this regard? First, stay away from foods like refined white breads, rice, and pasta that will clog the digestive system. Next, concentrate on fiber: To help those who are constipated, choose whole grains, such as fiber-rich cereals, and fresh fruit.

Another fantastic choice is dried fruit. Try all your favorite dried fruits, such as apples and blueberries, in addition to raw or lightly cooked vegetables, nuts, seeds, and that old people's favorite, prunes.

Third, drink plenty of liquids, especially water and juice, to wash that fiber down and through your system. V8 tastes exactly like champagne if you close your eyes! I guess, sort of.

Finally, keep in mind that moving around can keep things moving, which is another good reason to schedule exercise. Call your practitioner if things don't get better in a couple of days; he or she might have a few special tricks up that white-coated sleeve. Use only over-the-counter medications after consulting a physician.

Week 10 symptoms of pregnancy

Fatigue

Nausea and diarrhoea

Food aversions and cravings

Acid reflux and indigestion

Gas and bloating

Increased vulvar leaking

Periodic headaches

Dizziness or faintness

Observable veins

Tips for You This Week Regarding Round Ligament Pain

Take it easy during the ride

Uncontrollably crying one moment and laughing uncontrollably the next? These emotional ups and downs are typical of pregnancy.

With a break in the second trimester, mood swings are mostly felt during the first trimester. But beware—they frequently return during the final few months of pregnancy.

Prevent triggering odors

Avoid any smells that make you queasy as much as you can, whether they are the sausage and eggs your partner enjoys making on the weekends or the cologne or perfume that once had you head over heels but now has you running for the bathroom.

Avoid foods that you can't stand the sight of, as well. One frequent offender is raw chicken.

Consult your doctor regarding the COVID-19 vaccine.

Being pregnant puts you at a higher risk for COVID-19 complications, so it's a good idea to keep your distance from other people and cover your face when you're out in public, especially when you're inside.

The COVID-19 shot, which is currently offered to all adults, including pregnant women, may also be something you want to consider getting. But ultimately, it comes down to a personal choice. If you have any questions, consult your doctor.

Mention mangoes on your menu.

All fruits are healthy, but mangoes are especially beneficial for expectant mothers. Compared to a salad, they have more vitamins A and C per delicious bite.

Have a nutritious breakfast.

Oatmeal and DHA-enriched eggs are two breakfast options that are especially beneficial for your pregnant body and baby-building. If you haven't already, now is a good time to establish the habit of eating breakfast.

Oats are rich in iron, fiber, B vitamins, and a variety of other healthy minerals. Put them in your breakfast bowl, but don't stop there. Add oats to pancakes and muffins for all the nutritional benefits they provide (and cakes, cookies and even meatloaf).

It's great that you eat eggs. Still a good egg, the old one.

WEEK 11

EXPLORE WEEK 11 0f PREGNANCY

Your baby has developed distinct human features by week 11 of pregnancy, including fingers and toes!

As the first trimester comes to a close, some expectant mothers notice that their morning sickness begins to lessen. However, it's also common to still be feeling sick, have food aversions, and bloat at this time.

Baby has hands and feet in front of his body, ears that are almost finished developing, open nasal passages on the tip of his tiny nose, a tongue and palate in the mouth, and visible nipples by week 11 of pregnancy, among other distinctive human characteristics.

belly rumbling

It's good that you may be feeling a little more hungry these days. It's a sign that your morning sickness is lessening and that you are getting ready to eat more to nourish both yourself and your unborn child.

Just because you're feeding two people doesn't mean you should overeat. By selecting the healthiest foods possible and avoiding junk during pregnancy, you can try to gain weight efficiently.

Burping and bloating

The stomach and intestines will become more crowded as your uterus expands, increasing pressure on the digestive system and making you feel even more bloated.

Here is some solace: Baby won't experience your suffering. In fact, your baby is unaware of all of your intestinal discomfort and may even find comfort in the gurgling of your stomach.

By eating small, frequent meals rather than bingeing and avoiding foods that are known to cause gas, such as beans, fried foods, soda, and sweets, you can reduce bloating and gas.

pregnancy fatigue reduction

Eat energizing snacks like nuts, dried fruit, cheese, crackers, and other nutritious foods that can give you a boost to combat fatigue. Additionally, you should take cat naps whenever you can, stop when you're exhausted, and engage in pregnancy-safe exercises like walking to help fight the sleepiness.

11th week of pregnancy symptoms

often urinating

breast sensitivity and modifications

nausea and diarrhoea

Food aversions and cravings

Gas and bloating

dizziness or faintness

Advice for This Week

Pose in a manner

The ideal pregnancy exercise is prenatal yoga.

One prenatal yoga session per week for at least two months can significantly lower the risk of anxiety and depression, in addition to making you feel more at ease and prepared for birth. Premature birth and postpartum depression can be decreased as a result of this. hand cleaners.

Keep a smile on your face.

A new million-dollar smile may have to wait until after the birth of your million-dollar child. Although tooth whitening has no known risks, it is best avoided while you are pregnant because it is a procedure that is better to be safe than sorry.

But remember to regularly floss and keep your teeth clean. Pregnant women frequently experience gingivitis, or inflamed gums, so prevent it by chewing sugarless gum, which can help lessen plaque buildup, and snacking on nuts or cheese, which contain calcium and other nutrients.

Your extremely delicate gums will appreciate the care, and you'll also improve your chances of having a healthier pregnancy. Unexpectedly, poor dental hygiene has been connected to premature birth. And isn't a healthy mouth more crucial than pearly whites that are whiter?

Take your C.

Collagen, which supports your baby's cartilage, muscles, blood vessels, and bones, is made possible by vitamin C. Additionally, it enables a baby's body to repair wounded tissue.

Additionally, adequate vitamin C intake has been associated with a healthy birth weight and a lower risk of an early rupture of the membranes. Since vitamin C cannot be stored, you must ensure that you consume the recommended daily servings.

You can get your C by drinking vegetable juice and eating a variety of delicious fruits and vegetables, such as mangoes, cantaloupe, and strawberries, as well as the old standby of orange juice and oranges.

hydrate dry skin

Dry skin? Your skin can lose moisture if you take too many baths.

Don't worry if you're not in the mood.

Pregnancy symptoms can also get in the way of having fun; after all, it's difficult to feel sexy when you're too preoccupied to enjoy dinner.

Whatever is normal for you is normal, so don't worry. Keep in mind that a lot of women who lost their lust in the first trimester regain it in spades in the second... Therefore, if a very warm front moves into the bedroom soon, don't be shocked.

WEEK 12

EXPLORE WEEK 12 0f PREGNANCY

Your baby's intestines were encroaching on the umbilical cord during week 8 of pregnancy. However, they're finishing up the transition back into the abdomen this week.

Your baby is now the size of a lime, weighing a full half-ounce, and measuring 2 to 214 inches from crown to rump.

It's difficult to imagine — especially from the outside, as you're probably only just starting to show — but your baby has grown more than twice as big in the last three weeks.

the start of the digestive system in a baby

The organs begin to function and the systems of your fetus continue to develop over the next 28 weeks as it enters the maintenance phase. For starters, the fetal digestive system is starting to practice contraction movements, literally flexing its muscles. Your little peanut will need this ability after birth to push food through the digestive tract.

White blood cells, your baby's tools for fighting infection once she leaves your safe haven and joins a regular play group, are being produced by the bone marrow. Additionally, the hormones that will allow her to have children of her own in a few decades or so are already being produced by the pituitary gland at the base of the brain.

the cessation of some pregnancy side effects

If you're lucky, this will stop that annoying early pregnancy symptom of having to urinate all the time.

woozy episodes

Dizziness is a new pregnancy symptom that may be added to the list once you enter your second trimester.

Your blood pressure will drop, and less blood will flow through your body and to your brain as a result. Slow and steady wins the race in this situation because these factors can contribute to the light-headed, dizzy sensation, especially when you stand up too quickly.

Observational advice: If you experience lightheadedness or faintness, sit or lie down with your head between your knees, take a few deep breaths, and loosen any restrictive clothing, such as that button on your jeans that you had trouble fastening in the first place. Get some food and drink as soon as you start to feel better.

Low-quality drive

Every woman is affected by hormones differently, and for some, this results in an increase in sex desire while for others it lessens. Because it's difficult to get in the mood when you're sick, tired, or constipated (or all of the above and more!), pregnancy symptoms can also get in the way of having fun.

Whatever you're experiencing, don't worry; it's normal. Simply maintain an emotional connection with your partner and keep in mind that many pregnant women experience ups and downs in their sex drive. Consequently, a warmer period may soon arrive.

increased olfactory awareness

less frequent trips to the bathroom

Periodic headaches

Fatigue

Gas and bloating

a lot of saliva

Advice for This Week

Obtain a flu shot.

The Centers for Disease Control and Prevention (CDC) advises all expectant mothers to get vaccinated against the flu. Additionally, a recent study shows that being pregnant doesn't increase your risk for shot side effects.

begin executing Kegels

Your pelvic floor muscles must contract to previously unfathomable lengths in order to push your baby through your pelvis and into the world, which is demanding not only on you but also on them.

Exercises for the pelvic floor can reduce pregnancy symptoms and hasten postpartum recovery. Strive for three sets of 20 squeezes per day. Squeeze the pelvic floor muscles for up to 10 seconds.

Building these muscles that support your uterus and bladder lowers your risk of bladder problems and alleviates a variety of other pregnancy and postpartum symptoms.

Avoid drinking alcohol.

Beer, wine, and other alcoholic beverage bottles have warning labels on the sides for a reason. Alcohol consumption during pregnancy can have negative effects on the unborn child, including birth defects and other issues.

It's best to refrain from alcohol entirely until after delivery because even occasional drinking can lead to complications. However, if you drank a few drinks prior to learning you were pregnant, don't worry.

Reconsider hair removal

While shaving may be simple right now, as your pregnancy progresses you may find it difficult to maintain your balance or see below your belly.

. Even though taking a shower can make your skin and hair softer and easier to remove, always shave after you've finished because a mistake could be very costly.

If your skin isn't too sensitive, you might want to try waxing and sugaring as a long-term hair removal option (ask your doctor first if it's okay).

The verdict is still out on whether it's safe to use bleaches and hair removal creams and lotions during pregnancy, so think about putting them on hold until after you give birth.

Keep hydrated.

The water bottle is the one you should be aiming for. Staying hydrated is now more important than ever, so make sure to drink an additional glass of liquid for each half-hour of exercise without skipping a beat.

be aware of the foods to avoid

Fortunately, the Food and Drug Administration ensures that unpasteurized milk cannot be found in supermarkets (FDA).

However, you may come across soft cheeses that were produced using unpasteurized milk; these can contain pathogens like listeria.

Stick to hard cheeses or warm soft cheeses until bubbly for a safer alternative.

WEEK 13

EXPLORE WEEK 13 0f PREGNANCY

The baby's vocal cords and intestines are growing.

What else is happening inside? Tiny bones are starting to form in his arms and legs at 13 weeks pregnant. He can move them jerkily enough that he might be able to put his thumb in his mouth soon, a habit that could be useful forself-soothing when he's a newborn.

There will be significant changes to your baby's intestines as well. They had been expanding in a space inside the umbilical cord up until recently, but they have now relocated to your baby's abdomen, where they are now growing permanently and more conveniently. The placenta, which will eventually weigh 1 to 2 pounds at birth, is also growing to meet the needs of your developing fetus.

Your baby's vocal cords, which are the first step in learning to say, "I love you, Mommy!" are also developing this week. Obviously, you can't hear him cooing or crying just yet, but once he is born, you can be sure that little voice will be put to good use.

Do you feel more like you?

You should be feeling pretty good at this point in your pregnancy since you are 13 weeks along and one week away from the second trimester. After all, the second trimester isn't known for being the most comfortable and straightforward of the three.

But if you still don't feel well, don't worry. While the majority of your early pregnancy symptoms should be gone by now, some women experience nausea and fatigue that lasts into the fourth and even fifth months.

And unfortunately for some women, these symptoms as well as other common ones from the first trimester, like bloating, constipation, headaches, and breast tenderness, can last for part of the duration of pregnancy.

Virulent discharge

Your vaginal discharge may also have increased recently, which you may have noticed. This perfectly normal discharge, known as leukorrhea (try spelling that correctly in a spelling bee), is thin and milky in color, or mild-smelling, or occasionally even odourless

Additionally, it will probably get worse as your pregnancy goes on.

Leukorrhea is brought on by increased estrogen production and increased blood flow to the pelvic region. Its noble goal is to prevent infections from entering the birth canal and to maintain a balanced population of bacteria in the vagina. Unfortunately, leukorrhea can ruin your underwear in the process of achieving its noble objective.

Never use a tampon to stay dry; instead, use a panty liner if it makes you more comfortable. However, avoid doucheing while you are expecting because it can disturb the normal balance of microorganisms, cause vaginal infections, or even force air into the vagina, all of which can be harmful

Advice for This Week

Accept your sex drive.

The start of your second trimester often brings with it an increase in sex desire. Enjoy!

However, you might need to abstain if you've previously experienced early labor or miscarriage. Discuss your safe activity levels with your doctor.

Maintain your prenatal regimen.

Observe serving sizes.

Try not to overeat at mealtimes if you've been experiencing constipation. Large meals may overwork your digestive system and result in obstructions.

Instead of eating three large meals a day, try eating six smaller ones. Additionally, you might experience less bloating and gas this way.

sufficient calcium

It benefits a baby's developing body by strengthening the bones and teeth. However, calcium also benefits your body by preserving healthy bone density, preventing osteoporosis later in life, and reducing your risk of preeclampsia right now.

Therefore, be sure to consume milk and other foods high in calcium, such as broccoli, fortified juice, almonds, sesame seeds, soy products, green leafy vegetables, and salmon in cans.

Eat foods high in iron.

You're seriously in the blood-making business when you're having a baby. Since iron aids in the production of blood, you'll need plenty of it to keep your body's and your unborn child's supply of red healthy.

Eat more iron-rich foods like beef, duck, soy products, spinach, dried fruits, and potatoes with the skin on to increase your intake of this essential mineral. After week 20, your doctor might also advise taking a supplement to keep your iron levels stable as blood demand increases.

Leave some of your fruit unpeeled.

You're backed up, baby. Put an end to peeling apples and peaches.

One apple with the skin contains 4.4 grams of fiber, whereas one-half cup of applesauce only contains one gram.

Combat a cold

As if dealing with the symptoms of pregnancy weren't difficult enough, being pregnant makes you more susceptible to colds. Additionally, many medications that treat cold symptoms are contraindicated during pregnancy.

Drink plenty of liquids to recover more quickly. Warm drinks, such as ginger tea and chicken broth, are especially calming, but water and cold juices will also keep you hydrated.

WEEK 14

WELCOME TO THE SECOND TRIMESTER EXPLORE WEEK 14 0f PREGNANCY

Many expectant mothers start to feel more hungry, energized, and less queasy at 14 weeks pregnant as the early pregnancy symptoms start to pass.

Baby is straightening up.

They have become fluid, smooth, and balletic now.

In relation to ballet, it will be years before you start nagging your child to stand up straight, but amazingly, she is already doing so without your help! Your baby's neck is getting longer and helping her head stand more upright, so don't slouch any longer. Your fetus appears more straightened out as a result.

Baby's lanugo and sprouting hair

Additionally, your baby's mouth developed its own roof this week, and her digestive system began to function: Meconium, the waste that will make up her first bowel movement after birth, is being produced by her intestines.

painful round ligaments

Your OB/GYN might refer to round ligament pain as a possible side effect of uterine growth in some women. These are, in essence, pregnancy growing pains that feel like achy or sharp pains on one or both sides of the abdomen. They start to manifest around 14 weeks but can occur at any point in the second trimester.

This is why: Strong bands of ligaments that extend from the groin up the side of the abdomen support the uterus. The ligaments that support your uterus as it develops stretch and become thinner as it gets heavier. Your lower abdomen may feel either a sharp pain or a dull ache as a result of the weight pulling on the ligaments.

When you suddenly change positions, stand up from a sitting or lying down position, cough, or sneeze, it's frequently more obvious.

Which approach to relief is best? Put your feet up and relax in a cozy spot to relieve the stress and the pain.

maintaining health

As if dealing with the symptoms of pregnancy weren't difficult enough, being pregnant makes you more prone to getting the flu, the cold, and other viruses. Because your fetus is a foreign substance to your body, nature stifles your immune system during pregnancy to prevent it from being rejected.

The secret to staying healthy is to wage a little war on germs. The best offense is always the best defense, especially when contagious diseases are present.

Avoid sharing drinks, food, or toothbrushes, wash your hands frequently, carry liquid sanitizer with you for times when a sink is not available, and stay away from sick people at all costs. A sick spouse can be confined to the couch.

pregnancy symptoms

reducing weariness

increased breast size, decreased tenderness

Increasing hunger

dilated veins

clogged nose

nausea and vomiting disappearance

Advice for This Week

Track skin alterations

Because of the hormones associated with pregnancy, moles can grow or alter now.

However, having your doctor examine them is still a wise decision. To be safe, always talk to your doctor if you notice any changes in your skin.

Recall to eat

You should be aware that being hungry can actually make your nausea worse if you're avoiding food because you're still feeling sick. Fill your stomach gradually by beginning with liquids like water, fruit juices, smoothies, and soups, then add solids once you feel confident that your delicate stomach can handle them.

If you're still experiencing morning sickness, try eating small meals or snacks every two to three hours to help regulate your blood sugar levels and digestion.

Ignore the tattoos.

Thinking about getting a tattoo to mark your pregnancy? Think again. Even though only a small amount of the ink or its particles will enter your bloodstream, getting stabbed with a needle always carries the risk of infection.

Risky to take when trying to maintain your health for two.

Shop wisely at the supermarket

Think fresh, not processed, when you are grocery shopping. Fresh foods naturally contain more vitamins and minerals than processed foods, and they also have lower levels of sugar, salt, calories, fat, and additives.

The maxim "fresh is best" has one notable exception: When frozen fruits and vegetables aren't loaded with salt or sugar, they're frequently just as nutritious as fresh produce, if not more so. The same is true for canned food.

Select pregnancy-safe exercise equipment.

Play it cool when getting dressed for exercise success. During pregnancy, dress in loose, breathable, stretchy workout attire, down to your underwear (which should be cotton).

Choose a bra that gives your larger breasts plenty of support but doesn't pinch once you start moving, like a sports bra.

WEEK 15

EXPLORE WEEK 15 0f PREGNANCY

While your morning sickness might be gone by week 15 of pregnancy, you might be dealing with other uncomfortable symptoms like bleeding gums.

The months of gold

Baby now resembles a baby more.

Your fetus is also beginning to resemble the baby you envision in your dreams as each week goes by.

The eyes are moving from the side of the head to the front of the face, where they will soon meet, and the ears are now situated correctly on the sides of the head (they used to be in the neck).

Because he only weighs a few ounces, you won't feel the fetal movements taking place inside your abdominal gym. However, your fetus is also holding daily aerobics classes, kicking, curling toes, and moving those little arms and legs.

Gum disease and dental care

Say cheese and give your reflection a close examination. When you brush or floss, you might notice that your gums are red, swollen, and even painful, sensitive, or prone to bleeding. Once more, it's those pregnancy hormones at work, causing the gums to respond differently to the bacteria in plaque, causing gingivitis, an infection and inflammation.

What can happen if you don't take care of your teeth while you're expecting is a little more alarming. Periodontitis, an infection of the bones and tissues supporting your teeth, can develop from gingivitis, and studies have linked periodontitis to preterm labor and preeclampsia.

The key is prevention: Regular dental care, brushing at least twice a day, and gentle flossing once a day all contribute to good oral hygiene, which significantly reduces gum swelling, bleeding, and soreness.

Putting on weight

Your baby will continue to grow as you progress into the second trimester, so you should as well. Aim for a pound or so of weight gain each week and live by the motto "slow and steady wins the race."

But keep in mind that's an average, so as long as you're gaining about 4 pounds per month, it's fine to gain half a pound one week and a pound and a half the next. Just make sure to follow any advice your doctor gives you regarding weight gain.

pregnancy symptoms

Acid reflux and indigestion

dilated veins

dizziness or faintness

Periodic headaches

painful round ligaments

Advice on Pregnancy Brain This Week

Fit in nutritious food

Do you have trouble fitting in healthy meals to your schedule? Even if all you have for lunch is a sandwich and a fruit cup, you should adjust your schedule to make room for it.

Have a lot of healthy snacks on hand to make feeding you and your baby simple: Store a supply of individually wrapped cheese sticks, hard-boiled eggs, yogurt, and cottage cheese containers in the fridge, along with bags of dried fruit and nuts, dry cereal, and crackers.

Prioritize breakfast

Because you're not a breakfast person, do you skip breakfast? Your baby doesn't care if you choose a toasted cheese sandwich over the oatmeal or even a piece of the leftover cold meatloaf from last night's dinner.

If you skip breakfast because you're not a morning person, consider setting your alarm for 15 minutes earlier so you can wake up and grab some granola and yogurt, even if you have to eat it on the go.

If you're constantly pressed for time, try making something the night before, such as a breakfast burrito that only requires a quick microwave session or a bag of dry cereal and trail mix that can be consumed with calcium-fortified juice.

Make a quick breakfast smoothie by placing all the ingredients in the blender jar, storing it in the refrigerator, and then blending it in the morning.

Before exercising, eat.

The fact that exercise burns calories is one of its main advantages. However, you get the pleasure of replacing those calories with some wholesome pregnancy snacks because you are a card-carrying baby-builder.

So, grab a light snack and a drink from the refrigerator 30 minutes prior to working out. After your workout, have another snack.

Bananas and orange juice are excellent choices because they are high in potassium, a nutrient that is lost when you perspire and that is also necessary for quick energy. For added endurance, include some protein in the form of a cheese stick or a hard-boiled egg.

Inquire about aspirin

Preeclampsia typically appears later in pregnancy, after week 20, and is characterized by an abrupt increase in blood pressure, severe hand and face swelling, and indications that some organs may not be functioning normally, such as protein in the urine.

Ask your doctor about low-dose or baby aspirin if you are thought to be at high risk for preeclampsia. Preeclampsia can be decreased by 24% by taking baby aspirin (typically two a day, but check with your doctor) after the first trimester.

WEEK 16

EXPLORE PREGNANCY WEEK 16

vulnerable to light

This week, despite still being closed, your baby's eyes are making tiny side-to-side movements and are able to detect some light.

rapid expansion

At 16 weeks pregnant, your uterus is expanding pretty quickly, roughly at the same rate as your baby, and you may not be able to conceal your pregnancy any longer, even if you wanted to.

At this point, your baby is a whopping 3 to 4 ounces in weight and 4 to 5 inches long.

Your infant's back muscles and backbone are strengthening, allowing her to further straighten her head and neck.

In contrast to trimester one, you are probably still experiencing some degree of bliss in your second trimester, and in a few weeks, an ultrasound will allow you to see more of your unborn child.

nasal clogging

Not just your uterus but other organs are beginning to swell. The hormones associated with pregnancy that are circulating in your body and increasing blood flow can also affect the mucous membranes of your nose. The outcome?

Your nose is probably already aware of nasal congestion and even nosebleeds during pregnancy.

Unfortunately, the congestion might only worsen as your pregnancy goes on. Your doctor is unlikely to recommend any medications or antihistamine nasal sprays to help clear things up, so ask if they have any other recommendations.

Saline sprays or nasal strips are safe to use, particularly if the congestion becomes extremely uncomfortable. The dryness brought on by any congestion may also be relieved by a humidifier in your room and a small amount of petroleum jelly applied under your nose.

Week of Pregnancy Symptoms

continued breast development

Constipation

increased vulvar leaking

dilated veins

Backaches

bluish gums

Advice for This Week

Pick soups

Soups are a fantastic midday meal in any season. They can be as filling as you like, go well with other foods (think sandwiches), and are frequently rich in protein and fiber.

Make a double batch of soup so you can freeze some for later and enjoy them hot or cold.

Invest in cotton underwear instead

One of the first signs of pregnancy is frequently an increase in vaginal discharge, or leukorrhea in medical parlance. As your pregnancy progresses, the amount will probably rise as well because it is typically here to stay while you are expecting.

You shouldn't be concerned; this thin, white discharge is completely normal and healthy. Taking regular showers and donning breathable cotton underwear will suffice to keep the area dry and clean. Call your doctor if you have any concerns about what you are seeing.

Employ a humidifier

Around week 16 of your pregnancy, you usually start to experience that annoying stuffiness in your nose, as well as occasionally the nosebleeds that go along with it, especially if you're blowing frequently.

Sadly, they frequently persist and occasionally worsen right up until the end. To moisten your dry nose, try using a neti pot with bottled, distilled water and a humidifier.

When exercising, aim for healthy calories.

For every half hour of vigorous exercise, you get to eat an additional 100 to 200 calories when you're pregnant.

However, choose those calories wisely by consuming foods high in nutrients that won't negate the positive effects of all your hard work.

Try to refrain from grabbing the chocolate bar you were about to do. (That energy bar is probably also not much better.) Choose a smoothie, granola-yogurt parfait, some apple slices with almond or peanut butter, or whole grain crackers and cheese as an alternative.

Control back pain

Do you suffer from back pain? Try doing some light Pilates or yoga instead of nursing it on the couch. Both aid in releasing tension, which can be one of the main causes of back pain, and stretching and loosening the spine.

Yoga and Pilates also increase your overall energy and mood.

Additionally, you can perform easy exercises to strengthen your abdominal muscles, which will lessen the strain on your lower back. (However, keep in mind that since you are well into your second trimester, avoid exercising on your back.)

Choose greens

Make it a habit to always eat a side of salad, grilled vegetables, or sautéed leafy greens like broccoli, spinach, or escarole.

Likewise, tomato-based broths and chowders are excellent options, as are lentil, bean, and vegetable soups.

Obtain the quad screen ready

In a blood test known as a "quad screen," four substances that are produced by the fetus and the placenta and then transferred to the mother's bloodstream are measured.

The outcomes reveal your likelihood of carrying a child who has a chromosomal abnormality or neural tube defect.

Results from the nuchal translucency (NT) screening and noninvasive prenatal testing (NIPT) can be combined with those from the quad screen to provide you with a more accurate evaluation.

WEEK 17

EXPLORE WEEK 17 0f PREGNANCY

During the second trimester, around week 17 is when pregnancy vertigo frequently begins. Blame hormones, a developing uterus, and a circulatory system that is expanding quickly.

Your infant is simultaneously learning to suck and swallow and beginning to form fingerprints. How much your infant has grown! Your infant is the size of your palm, or about 5 inches long, and weighs 5 or more ounces. Join the club, baby, as your baby's body fat is starting to form and will keep building up until your pregnancy is over.

Baby's heart is beating at 140 to 150 beats per minute, which is roughly twice as fast as yours, and is now controlled by the brain, so there are no longer any erratic beats.

Your increasing hunger

Do you recall the time you were so queasy you could hardly drink any ginger ale or eat a cracker? You can rejoice that your nights and days of toilet-hugging are probably over. And fortunately, you're now more likely to experience food insecurity.

Most women experience relief from morning sickness and an increase in appetite during the second trimester. At 17 weeks pregnant, don't be shocked if you find yourself suddenly famished enough to devour a substantial piece of steak or an entire tray of baked ziti.

What's causing your appetite to grow? To put it simply, you are listening to your baby's growing and growing hunger. Uncertain of the precise amount of weight you should put on while pregnant? Speak with your doctor, who can assist you in sustaining a healthy weight gain. If you didn't gain enough weight or lost weight during the first trimester, your doctor or midwife can also assist you in playing catch-up with your weight gain.

Quit snoring.

Snoring is one strange pregnancy symptom! But don't worry; the stuffiness that frequently causes world-champion snoring is normal and will pass. Yes, pregnancy hormones have an impact on even your nose!

Consider installing a humidifier in your bedroom, using one of those nasal strips to widen your nasal passages, or elevating your head on a few pillows while you sleep. What if your spouse raises an issue? You should prioritize getting a good night's sleep over banishing your sweetheart to the couch for the evening.

increased symptoms

This week, you might experience an increase in vaginal discharge (leukorrhea), as well as a greater sensitivity to allergens. Both are entirely typical.

17th week of pregnancy symptoms

higher appetite

higher appetite

Stretch stains

Periodic headaches

dizziness or faintness

Acid reflux and indigestion

Backaches

Advice for This Week

Normal breast development (and absence of breast development)

To get ready for nursing, hormones and milk-producing glands are developing. Your breasts may enlarge by up to three cup sizes as a result of all this activity and an increase in blood flow.

Of course, a pregnant woman will experience different symptoms. Although breast growth is common, and for some women quite significant, you might not notice any changes in your breast size at all, especially if you are already very busty. If you don't have any breast growth, it's not a problem.

To prevent sciatica, stretch

The largest nerve in the body, the sciatic, originates in the lower back, travels down the buttocks, and branches off to the ankles and feet on the backs of the legs.

Most often, sciatica occurs when this nerve is compressed by bulging, slipped, or ruptured discs. Sciatica is characterized by sharp, shooting pain, tingling, or numbness that begins in the back or buttocks and radiates down the legs.

Other causes include arthritis and spinal stenosis, a narrowing of the spinal canal. To relieve pain, try stretching your back or using a heating pad.

The tooth fairy should return soon.

Particularly if you have more severe untreated conditions like gingivitis or periodontis, hormones can have an adverse effect on the gums, ligaments, and bones in your mouth, which in turn can cause a slight loosening of the teeth.

Don't put off visiting the dentist if you notice a very loose tooth or have other serious dental problems. Additionally, remember to maintain your regular flossing, twice-daily brushing, and other crucial oral hygiene routines throughout your pregnancy.

Reduce ring ligament pain

Thick bands (also known as ligaments) that extend from the groin up the side of the abdomen support your uterus.

These bands expand as your uterus expands during pregnancy to accommodate your expanding bump, which can result in sharp pains and dull aches in the lower abdomen.

Make sure to spend time off your feet and reduce the intensity of your workouts to relieve round ligament pain. For a little extra support, you might also think about donning a belly band.

Keep away from the sun

Are there any spots on your face? a slash down the middle of your belly? Are there skin tags on your upper arms?

No rush to the dermatologist is necessary. All of these odd skin symptoms, such as darkening moles and heat rashes, are normal and transient. Hormones are once again to blame, but the sun can make these changes in your complexion worse.

So stay shaded whenever you can — now's the time to invest in a wide-brimmed hat — and apply a broad spectrum sunscreen with an SPF of 30 or higher when you venture out in the daylight. <u>Sunscreen is safe</u> and smart to use when you're expecting. Ask your doctor about anything you're concerned about.

Check your hands

Do the palms of your hands look as if you've touched a hot pan? You could have <u>palmar erythema</u>, a skin condition in which the palms of the hands or the soles of the feet appear redder or darker than normal.

The good news: It disappears after you give birth. But definitely check in with your doctor just to make sure everything is normal.

Try calcium-rich, non-dairy foods.

If milk or other dairy products are not your thing, you will need to find another way to benefit from calcium. Fortunately, dairy products aren't the only calcium sources; they're just the most popular.

When compared cup for cup, calcium-fortified orange juice and other fruit juices can provide about as much calcium as milk. Leafy green vegetables, sesame seeds, almonds, and calcium-fortified soy products like tofu are other non-dairy dietary sources of calcium.

You still don't have enough. To provide additional protection, inquire with your doctor about a calcium supplement.

WEEK 18

EXPLORE WEEK 18 0f PREGNANCY

Recognize a rumbling in your stomach?

Pregnancy hunger pangs may be the cause, or it may be the very first fetal movement signs, which can appear around week 18 of pregnancy.

How much does my baby weigh at 18 weeks?

Your baby may be big enough now or anytime in the next few weeks for you to feel twisting, rolling, kicking, and punching in the womb. Your baby is 512 inches long from crown to rump and weighs 5 to 612 ounces, which is about the size of that boneless chicken breast you're making for dinner.

The back hurts.

Back pain is another thing you might be experiencing right now. Your center of gravity changes as your uterus grows —which causes your lower back to be pulled forward while your abdomen is thrust out. This is bad for your back muscles and good for alerting the person who got the last seat on the bus that you are pregnant.

You develop backaches and pains as a result of this, in addition to the changes that the pregnancy hormone relaxin is enacting, such as relaxing all of your ligaments, including those that attach your pelvic bones to your spine, and loosening joints. You may also notice a change in your posture.

When seated, elevate your feet with a foot rest to lessen pain. To relieve some of the strain on your lower back while standing, try to prop one foot up on a low stool. A long, warm bath can be extremely beneficial.

And be sure to consult your doctor if your back pain just won't go away.

reducing acid reflux

Forget the burrito with extra jalapenos; these days, sometimes even a bite of toast can make your stomach burn. That is the issue with heartburn, a symptom that is all-too-common and can last the duration of your pregnancy. Although you might want to keep those on hand as well since they'll eliminate the burn while increasing your calcium intake, an ounce of prevention may be worth a pound of Tums.

Eat slowly and chew each bite thoroughly to start. Eat smaller meals and snacks instead of five-alarm gut bombs, and try to avoid eating lunch on the run or devouring your dinner while sitting up.

After eating, stay upright for a few hours, or for as long as you can stand before falling asleep in bed, and sleep with your head elevated to reduce snoring. And steer clear of anything on the menu that has a flame-related image next to it!

Week 18 of Pregnancy Symptoms

Fetal motion

Gas and bloating

Leg twitches

bluish gums

Edema (swelling in feet and ankles)

Stretch stains

Advice for This Week

Avoid making any quick movements.

Progesterone increases blood flow to the developing fetus during pregnancy, which lowers blood pressure and reduces blood flow to the brain, giving you a general feeling of weakness.

Always get out of a sitting or lying position slowly to prevent dizziness.

Consult with pediatricians

You should schedule interviews with potential pediatricians right now in your pregnancy. After all, there's a good chance that your baby will visit the doctor for the first time within 24 hours of birth.

Therefore, before you choose, ask lots of questions and bring up issues like the availability of appointments, hospital affiliations, vaccinations, and circumcision.

It's time to unwind.

Sadly, we do not mean to be "relaxing." Your body produces the hormone relaxin during the second trimester, which loosens the ligaments that connect your bones. The outcome: sore hips and pelvis, possibly even bigger feet!

When you're trying to push out your baby's large head, you may be cursing the pregnancy hormone relaxin right now, but you'll be grateful that it did its job.

Iron pump

Even people who consume a lot of red meat may have trouble getting enough iron from their diets. You'll need to work twice as hard to increase your iron intake if you only eat plant-based foods because pregnant vegan and vegetarian women are more likely to develop iron deficiency anemia.

Even though foods like spinach, seaweed, Jerusalem artichokes, beans, soy products, oat bran, barley, pumpkin seeds, dried fruits, and blackstrap molasses all contain some iron, you might also need to take an iron supplement to make sure you're getting your recommended daily allowance. Check with your doctor to see if that is the case.

Watch out for supplements

When you have few options for self-medication during pregnancy, herbal supplements do seem like the most alluring option. Would taking a few ginkgo biloba capsules really hurt you if you wanted to give your brain cells a better chance of remembering to pay the electric bill this month? The bottles do say "all natural" after all, and you did purchase them from a health food store.

Actually, it might hurt, especially now that you're giving the child another pill. The Food and Drug Administration (FDA) does not test or approve herbs or herbal remedies before they are placed on the market, and they are not required to go through clinical trials, making it impossible to determine whether they are safe or not.

Additionally, a number of herbs, including sassafras, wild yam, black or blue cohosh, clove oil, and many others, can be extremely harmful if taken at any point during pregnancy. Before taking any medication, exercise caution and speak with your doctor.

Avoid certain exercises

Don't even consider trying some exercises that might be great for the non-pregnant set now that you're expecting.

After the fourth month, just refrain from doing shoulder stands, upside-down "bicycles," or lying flat on your back.

Deep knee bends, back bends, jumping, and bouncing are also prohibited.

Prepare for little kicks

The first tiny kicks from the baby will likely appear between weeks 18 and 22; for first-time pregnancies, this can sometimes happen as late as weeks 23 or 24.

A miscalculated due date can also affect how those historic first kicks are remembered. Don't worry; once your baby masters the technique and grows big enough to deliver a serious punch, there's no mistaking the real thing.

WEEK 19

EXPLORE WEEK 19 0f PREGNANCY

Vernix creates

This week, your child might get a cheesy varnish.

Whoa, what? Vernix caseosa, a protective substance, was what you just read (vernix is the Latin word for "varnish"; caseosa means "cheese")

You might see your baby's first anti-wrinkle cream as the vernix sheds as delivery nears, but some babies, particularly those born early, will still be covered with it at birth.

Leg twitches

During the second and third trimesters, these excruciating spasms that radiate up and down your calves are extremely frequent. These cramps can happen during the day, but you'll notice them more at night — oh, baby, will you notice them! Nobody is certain of their exact cause.

Whatever the cause, if a leg cramp does occur, you'll need a quick fix, especially if it prevents you from getting a good night's sleep. And now for one for you: Flex your ankle and toes back gently while straightening your leg.

Detecting the baby's kicks

Those first fetal movements may sometimes feel like bufferflies in your stomach, while other times you may feel like something is swimming inside of you (which it is!).

You won't be able to mistake those tiny kicks for anything else once your baby gets bigger and you can easily tell what they feel like.

higher appetite

Stretch stains

Constipation

Dizziness or faintness

Backaches

Clogged nose

Advice for This Week

Check for yeast infections

The last thing you need when you're pregnant and have a lot going on down there is an itchy yeast infection. Unfortunately, because of increased estrogen levels that lead to yeast overgrowth during pregnancy, you're more likely to get them.

Another drawback is that yeast infections are more challenging to treat at this time. Ask your doctor for advice on the best course of action.

Think about support hose

Purchasing a pair of support hose might be helpful if you struggle with edema, or swelling. Good options include knee- or thigh-highs that aren't too tight on top or full pantyhose (with extra belly room). They work better if you put them on in the morning before the daily swelling begins.

A comfortable pair of shoes is also beneficial for edema, as well as for leg and back pain during pregnancy.

Reevaluate 3D ultrasounds

Although there is no solid scientific proof that ultrasounds harm a fetus in development, there are still unknown risks associated with the technology. Only licensed medical professionals should conduct ultrasounds, according to the American College of Obstetricians and Gynecologists (ACOG), and only for medical purposes. So, despite how alluring they may seem, stay away from the elective ones for the time being.

progressively up your fiber intake

When you need to go, eating a healthy amount of fiber can help. The drawback is that consuming too much fiber quickly can result in gas, cramping, and bloating (and let's face it, you probably already have enough of those symptoms).

If you're trying to consume more fiber than ever, increase your intake gradually and subtly. For instance, add chia seeds to your morning cereal or have a trail mix snack in the afternoon to give your body time to get used to the new routine.

Fill out your pillows.

Even though you may not have snored before becoming pregnant, you are having trouble sleeping.

Snoring is typically more bothersome than harmful during pregnancy (it's typically brought on by an increase in nasal congestion, which can begin around week 16), but on rare occasions, it may be brought on by a long-term condition called obstructive sleep apnea. Ask your doctor about it and get advice on what to do

Build a sandwich.

No matter what kind of sandwich you prefer—wraps, paninis, double-deckers—make it a healthy one by adding lean protein, fiber, and whole grains. Fill it to the brim with greens to make the most of your lunch.

Simply avoid any sprouts because they can harbor bacteria and substitute more inventive lunch meats instead of traditional lunch meats that contain nitrates and nitrites.

Keep the action going

Water, vegetable or fruit juice, or broth in eight to ten full glasses per day will help keep solids moving through your digestive tract quickly and keep your stools soft and simple to pass.

Due to its mild laxative properties, prune juice is the best in the category. When you're really congested, try to drink some; if you find it difficult to do so, combine it with other fruits and juices to make a smoothie.

Another tried-and-true method for getting things moving is to drink warm liquids, such as the hot water and lemon that is a staple of health spas. They'll aid in promoting peristalsis, those bowel contractions that aid in urination.

WEEK 20

EXPLORE WEEK 20 0f PREGNANCY

You are already halfway through your pregnancy at 20 weeks along!

This week, the baby's lungs are growing more.

There is still plenty of room for growth inside your baby's body, allowing him to twist and turn (and letting you feel his acrobatics!).

You've reached the halfway point of your pregnancy (20 weeks down, 20 more to go!), and now that you can feel the movements of your unborn child and see the smiles of onlookers thanks to your growing baby bump, it's starting to feel more real.

growth of hair and nails

You might also notice that your hair feels fuller and thicker than usual, and that your nails are stronger than usual. Once more, you can thank pregnancy hormones for causing a spike in circulation that carries extra nutrients to the cells of your hair and nails.

Your nails may be long, but they can also become brittle and dry over time. Don't get too attached, even though you may adore your luxurious locks right now: Your streak of good hair days comes to an end after delivery, when the daily hair loss that is typically suppressed during pregnancy (hence the thicker mane) resumes and then some.

satiating your expanding appetite

You might be in the Hunger Zone. You may be more than ready to make up for lost eating time now that weeks of nausea and food aversions are behind you — say goodbye to crackers and hello to four-course meals!

According to studies, mothers who consume at least five small meals and snacks throughout the day are more likely to carry their babies to term.

So when the urge to eat strikes during pregnancy, eat lots of food and do so gradually.

20th week of pregnancy symptoms

Acid reflux and indigestion

Periodic headaches

dizziness or faintness

Leg twitches

Edema (swelling in feet and ankles)

Your good deed turns bad

Advice for This Week

Create a baby registry.

You haven't yet started a baby registry. A registry will help you keep track of all the equipment you need before your child arrives, whether you're having a baby shower or shopping for yourself. Most retailers offer freebies, discounts, and other benefits when you sign up, so lots of expectant parents register for several gift ideas. With What to Expect's Registry Builder, you can keep track of all your registries in one location.

Stretch without going too far

The stretching of muscles and loosening of ligaments, which makes them more vulnerable to injury, is one of the many symptoms of pregnancy.

When exercising, keep that in mind and stretch sensibly but not excessively. Stop moving if it hurts. Furthermore, even if it doesn't hurt, this is not the time to attempt a split.

Prevent anemia

Your body's reserve of stored iron, which you built up when your periods stopped, is almost gone by week 20 of pregnancy. However, your developing baby is currently in the greatest need of fresh red blood cells. You run the risk of having low iron levels, or anemia.

Although all expectant mothers are at risk for anemia, those who have recently given birth, are carrying multiple fetuses, or have ever been malnourished during their pregnancies are at even higher risk.

How can those supplies be increased? Discuss with your doctor whether you should take an iron supplement, and eat foods high in iron along with foods high in vitamin C, such as a red pepper and steak stir-fry, as an example.

Elect for oil-free skin care.

When purchasing cosmetics and skin care items, search for the terms "non-comedogenic," "unscented," and "oil-free." They'll be less likely to add excessive oils and clog pores, which is advantageous if your skin is already oily. However, it is best to choose moisturizing products if your skin is dry.

Give nuts a try

Enjoy nuts? Continue to eat them!

The risk of nut allergies in your unborn child is not increased by eating nuts while you are pregnant; in fact, it may be decreased.

Vitamin E, protein, and vital minerals like copper, manganese, magnesium, selenium, zinc, potassium, and even calcium are all abundant in nuts.

Even though they contain a lot of fat, most of it is healthy, especially the AHA that helps develop the baby's brain. In summary, have fun, but only in moderation.

WEEK 21

EXPLORE WEEK 21 0f PREGNANCY

It makes sense that you might feel more kicking and stretching at 21 weeks pregnant because your baby has more control over limb movements.

Stretch marks, which can appear as your belly grows, can leave pink, red, purple, reddish-brown, or dark brown streaks on the outside that your child may be leaving behind.

How much does my baby weigh at 21 weeks?

What size is your infant? He measures 1012 inches from crown to rump to crown to heel, or about the size of a large banana, and weighs 11 to 1212 ounces.

Although, like anyone who has lived in one place for a long time, your developing baby still has plenty of room in your womb, this tenant will soon start to feel crowded.

Stretch stains

At 21 weeks pregnant, your baby may be beginning to leave his mark on your stomach, butt, thighs, hips, and breasts in the form of stretch marks.

As your body enlarges and your tummy and breasts continue to grow, pink, red, purple, reddish-brown, or dark brown streaks start to show up: The supporting tissue beneath your skin tears as the skin stretches.

Reducing worry

Almost every expectant parent experiences anxiety and fear at some point in their pregnancy, usually once that pregnancy becomes a very visible reality. It's almost as if you're on a runaway train and there are big changes coming around the corner.

Additionally, acknowledging your anxiety is particularly beneficial. Feeling anxious is completely normal. Discuss your emotions with your friends who have children; they will reassure you that they had similar feelings. Most importantly, talk about your fears with your partner, if you have one, as they likely need to talk about them as well.

Week of Pregnancy Symptoms

Fetal motion

higher appetite

Gas and bloating

Backaches

bluish gums

rapid-growth nails

Advice for This Week

Decongest your nose.

Use your thumb to cover one nostril and gently blow out the other to clear your nasal passages. Repeat on the other side after that. Ask your doctor if there is a safe over-the-counter decongestant or antihistamine you can use if you are really congested.

Raise your feet.

You're having more trouble than usual tying your shoes. It could be due to swollen ankles and feet. Your extremities are more prone to swelling because your body has about 50% more blood and fluid than it did before having a baby. A few sit-and-elevate sessions should therefore be scheduled throughout the day.

30 minutes a day of walking

Are your pipes clogged? Afterward, begin walking for exercise. Physical activity, like a brisk walk, is one of the best ways to stimulate your bowels and fight constipation, both during pregnancy and in those first few weeks after giving birth.

Even just a half-hour stroll each day can be effective, especially if you consume lots of water and choose foods high in fiber. When you hit the trail, just don't forget to bring some trail mix. Walking is a great way to get the exercise you need when you're pregnant, even if you're not doing it to relieve constipation or other pregnancy symptoms.

Eliminate lasers

Because of all those raging hormones, you might have more hair than usual on your legs, armpits, bikini line, and upper lip. However, think twice before using bleaching, depilatory drugs, lasers, or electrolysis.

But don't worry; you can shave or pluck to your heart's content. Waxing is also acceptable if your skin is not overly sensitive. That's not improving your mood, is it? Keep your head up; you've already passed the halfway point.

Get your calendar ready.

You're not forgetting where you put your keys because you didn't get enough sleep, though that certainly doesn't help. Forgetfulness and difficulty concentrating are two symptoms of brain fog, which is a common pregnancy symptom.

Now is the time to start creating to-do lists, leaving notes for yourself in obvious places, and outsourcing some of your regular tasks to your partner or non-pregnant friends and family because so-called "pregnancy brain" may very well be here to stay for the duration of your pregnancy.

Eat fewer empty calories

"Empty" is stressed. You still need to eat enough nutrients to support your baby's growth and maintenance. After all, losing weight is never a good idea when you're pregnant. The goal is to maintain a healthy weight.

it is to maintain a healthy diet and slow and steady weight gain.

Simple dietary changes, such as switching to fresh fruit instead of dried, baked potatoes or yams instead of French fries, and grilling white meat chicken without the skin rather than deep-frying dark meat with the skin, can have a significant impact.

Other calories you could cut? the ones that are present in sweet treats.

WEEK 22

EXPLORE WEEK 22 0f PREGNANCY

The grip, vision, and hearing of your infant are all now developing more.

As a result of the hormones and pregnancy swelling, you may also be noticing additional changes, such as a protruding navel and possibly even slightly larger feet (called edema). Your infant, who resembles a small doll in size, has at last reached the 1-pound milestone.

This Week's Tips for Your Protruding Navel

Getting better with practice

Is your uterus getting ready to give birth? It is if your abdomen experiences irregular, painless, squeezing sensations. These contractions are Braxton Hicks contractions, which are not harmful. They resemble a dress rehearsal somewhat: Your uterine muscles are tensing up in anticipation of the significant task they will have to complete soon.

Remember that while they may be difficult to distinguish from the real thing, only actual labor contractions are effective enough to push your baby out.

Inquire about fFN screenings

A preterm birth risk? A fetal fibronectin (fFN) test might be performed by your doctor. A protein called FFN is created during pregnancy and functions as a kind of "glue" to keep the baby in your uterus.

If the results are bad, you're not at risk, but if they're good, your chances of having an early labor increase. If so, your doctor might take measures to extend your pregnancy and get your baby's lungs ready for a preterm delivery.

Your friend is magnesium.

Magnesium, a mineral present in pumpkin seeds, chia seeds, almonds, and cashews, works to stimulate enzyme function, regulate insulin, and control blood sugar levels in addition to strengthening baby's bones and teeth.

Make sure you're getting enough magnesium from your diet and prenatal vitamins by speaking with your doctor. If you're depressed, you might experience leg cramps or restless legs, feel exhausted and lack muscle strength (as if you needed any more of that these days).

Schedule a workout

You're not the only one who benefits from a sweat session, according to scientific research. Pregnant women who exercise during their pregnancies have babies who, on average, perform better on IQ tests by the age of 4. Your workout will increase not only your muscle power but also the brain power of your unborn child!

Pause to breathe

Learning some calming relaxation techniques is a great idea right now, not only because they can help you deal with pregnancy anxieties (and later, labor contractions), but also because they'll be useful to you as a new mom when the baby is having a crying fit.

Close your eyes and picture a stunning, tranquil scene, such as a sunset over your preferred beach or a peaceful mountain vista.

Next, focus on relaxing every muscle as you move up from your toes to your face.

Select a simple word (like "yes" or "one") to say out loud with each exhalation as you take a slow, deep breath through your nose. It should only take ten minutes, but even a minute or two is preferable to nothing.

WEEK 23

EXPLORE WEEK 23 0f PREGNANCY

Prepare for a significant growth spurt; starting this week, your baby's size will likely double over the course of the next few weeks.

Additionally, you might begin to experience the foggy, hazy feeling known as "pregnancy brain" as a result of the pregnancy hormones being in overdrive.

One remedy? Make post-it notes your friend and place tiny reminders around the house where you'll see them.

How much do I weigh at 23 weeks?

This week marks the start of some serious weight gain, with the puppy measuring about 11 inches long and weighing just over a pound.

Over the course of the next four weeks, your baby should double in weight, and you might feel the same way.

new signs appear

Your mind is foggy (this is your brain...this is your brain on progesterone) and your feet are expanding at 23 weeks pregnant. You might have reddened palms and soles, and you might be more prone to heat rash and skin tags.

On practically every available skin surface, stretch marks are blooming in vivid hues of pink, red, purple, reddish-brown, or dark brown. But wait! What's up with that strange dark line that runs down the middle of your belly?

coloration of the skin

It's referred to as the "dark line," or linea nigra, believe it or not. The linea nigra, which runs between your belly button and your pubic region, is a typical pregnancy sign that may be easier to see in women with darker skin.

The same pregnancy hormones that cause all other skin discolorations, including the darker shade of your areolas and the deeper tone of the freckles on your arms and legs, are also to blame for this one.

Many women, particularly those with darker skin, also notice discoloration on the face, particularly in the cheeks, eyes, forehead, and nose region. Because it has a mask-like appearance on the face, it is known as the pregnancy mask (or melasma).

You won't be playing masquerade for very long, rest assured. After delivery, all of these skin alterations will disappear. Bring on the concealer in the interim, but skip the bleaching creams, which are ineffective anyway.

Fetal motion

robust appetite

Bloating\sSnoring

bluish gums

Tickled hands

Advice for This Week

What is the key to a restful night's sleep?

Getting a good night's sleep while pregnant can be nearly as difficult as it is when you first become a parent. In fact, a staggering 78 percent of pregnant women report having sleep issues at one point or another, according to one study.

With everything going on in your body and brain, it is understandable why getting a good night's sleep can be difficult. If you're having trouble relaxing, try putting a pillow between your legs and taking a seat with your knees bent.

inquiry regarding maternity leave

It's time to start planning for maternity leave even though you have still got a few weeks before meeting the baby. Connect with HR and your manager to make sure you all understand the details and are on the same page.

Refill the water in your bottle.

Always keep a bottle of water close at hand. Drinking enough water keeps your extra blood volume in check, replenishes amniotic fluid, and increases milk production.

Take action to avoid UTIs

Your bladder now serves as the ideal breeding ground for bacteria because it is being squeezed by your expanding uterus, which can result in a urinary tract infection (UTI). Fortunately, there are many ways to lower your risk of getting a UTI while pregnant.

Drink plenty of water and cranberry juice, preferably one without added sugar (though the second remedy has mixed results).

If your urine is dark and not straw-colored, you may not be drinking enough fluids and be putting yourself at risk for a UTI.

Other advice: If you can find a bathroom, urinate as soon as you feel the urge. When you use the restroom, focus on completely emptying your bladder, and try to lean forward as you urinate. From front to back, wipe.

Lastly, especially after having sex, clean your genitalia and the areas around them. When possible, use only cotton underwear and avoid baths in favor of showers.

Rethink hair treatments

Have you considered having your hair straightened or curled at a salon now that you are past the first trimester? You might want to think twice.

Give organic products a shot

Filling your plate with fresh fruits and vegetables, whether they are organic or not, is always a good idea.

Additionally, artificial preservatives, colorings, and flavors are not used in organic foods. Organic produce can sometimes have a shorter shelf life and is more expensive than conventional fruits and vegetables.

Remember, choosing a wide variety of nutrient-dense foods and fresh, ripe fruits and vegetables in a variety of hues is what's most crucial. Additionally, you must thoroughly wash all of your produce in cold water, whether you purchase conventional or organic fruits and vegetables.

Do Pilates.

Everyone is doing it, including their pregnant neighbor, but is Pilates the best form of exercise for you? Yes, and it's not a stretch!

When you exercise for two, you need to strengthen your core and lengthen your muscles, which is exactly what this mind-body discipline focuses on doing.

If you're a beginner, be careful not to attempt any of the moves on your own. It is best to perform them under the supervision of a Pilates instructor, preferably one with experience in prenatal exercises.

WEEK 24

EXPLORE WEEK 24 0f PREGNANCY

Such a face! Your baby's facial features are starting to take shape at 24 weeks pregnant. If things keep up, your baby will be ready for all the pictures you'll take after giving birth!

Your baby is currently 1 pound, 1112 inches long, and growing at a consistent rate of roughly 6 ounces per week. A large portion of that weight is caused by developing bones, muscles, organs, and baby fat.

belly button adjustments

Welcome to the club if you used to be an indie but are now an outie. A pregnant woman's belly button almost always pops at some point as the growing uterus pushes against everything in its path.

After giving birth, everything should return to normal, though your navel and some other body parts might appear a little, um, stretched. Consider it just another badge of honor that only mothers can don.

Palmar-plantar syndrome

Carpal tunnel syndrome affects pregnant women for a different reason, though repetitive motion can certainly contribute. Carpal tunnel syndrome is characterized by the uncomfortable tingling and numbness you notice in your wrists and fingers.

Pregnancy-related swelling causes fluid to build up in your lower extremities throughout the day. When you're lying down, the fluid is then redistributed to the rest of your body, including your hands, which puts pressure on the nerve that runs through your wrist. That makes the fingers, hand, or wrist numb, tingly, painful, or achy.

Avoid sleeping on your hands and elevate your arms with a pillow at night to find relief. Shaking your wrists and hands could also be beneficial. Make sure to take frequent hand-stretching breaks if you are performing repetitive motions, such as playing the piano or typing, as these activities can exacerbate your symptoms.

A wrist brace might be the answer to your pain relief needs if you're in a lot of discomfort. Fortunately, the carpal tunnel syndrome symptoms disappear as well when the normal swelling of pregnancy stops after delivery.

calming red, irritated palms

You may have heard that pregnancy has a number of symptoms, most of which are unpleasant. Well, unless you count your breasts, hair, and nails growing quickly.

However, perhaps you weren't prepared for so many bizarre symptoms, like the red, itchy palms that have nothing to do with how much dishwashing you're doing. The soles of your feet may also turn red, though you won't likely notice that once it's harder to see your feet.

Even though this is a symptom that is generally considered to be normal, particularly this far along in pregnancy, be sure to mention it to your doctor because there is a chance that it might signify a rare pregnancy complication called cholestasis, though this is more common in the third trimester.

Applying an ice pack for a few minutes a few times per day or soaking their hands and feet in cold water can provide relief for some women.

While you're expecting, you might even try going on a dishwashing strike; just make sure to tell your spouse it's a doctor's order.

pregnancy symptoms

Constipation

lower-back discomfort

distorted vision

Migraines

Leg twitches

enlarged ankles and feet

Advice for This Week

Prepare for the glucose test.

Between 24 and 28 weeks, your doctor will perform a glucose screening on you. You'll probably need to change your diet, monitor your blood sugar at home, and possibly increase your activity levels if your blood sugar levels reveal that you have gestational diabetes, a temporary condition that manifests during pregnancy.

Researchers do not yet fully understand why some women develop gestational diabetes while others do not, but they do know that certain risk factors, such as being overweight, are older, are expecting multiples, have a family history of diabetes, or are pregnant with multiples.

Shorten your showers

experiencing dry skin while pregnant? Your skin can lose moisture if you take too many baths.

Stick to quick showers—which are good practice for motherhood—in warm water—not hot—and use a gentle cleanser. Try a moisturizer or install a warm-mist humidifier in your room if you have extremely dry skin.

Prepare some meals.

Your freezer is a friend; cook just once and put plenty of wholesome leftovers in it.

The same principle applies to soups and stews: prepare a large quantity, freeze it in single-serve containers, and then reheat it later for a filling snack. Similar to mini meat loaves,

Cut up enough fruit salad or vegetables to last you for days while still allowing you to enjoy a healthy diet. Additionally, grill four or more chicken breasts rather than just one; the leftovers will make delectable sandwiches, dinnertime salad toppings, or fajita fillings in the days to come.

You don't have to do it alone, by the way. Make it a group effort by asking for assistance from your partner, if you have one, as well as from your family, friends, neighbors, and even other children, if this isn't your first child.

Hemorrhoids' sting can be lessened.

After a bowel movement, use warm water and white two-ply toilet paper to keep it clean. Avoid using the toilet for too long or using too much force when wiping. Change to wipes (preferably those made with plain water or intended for sensitive skin) if TP is too harsh.

Take a warm (not hot) bath to help you feel better.

WEEK 25

EXPLORE WEEK 25 0f PREGNANCY

Your uterus is now about the size of a soccer ball, and you may finally have the noticeable baby bump you've been picturing since the beginning of your pregnancy now that you're in week 25.

Your baby's nose and lungs are also developing more fully in preparation for life outside the womb.

Your baby has grown tremendously, measuring 13 inches long, or over a foot, and weighing more than 112 pounds.

That is nearly as heavy as four juice boxes and is taller than two juice boxes stacked on top of one another.

Hemorrhoids

Due to the larger uterus pressing down and the increased blood flow to the area, more than half of pregnant women experience swollen, itchy veins in the rectum. And while hemorrhoids, a type of varicose veins, are not harmful to your body, they can be excruciatingly painful and even result in rectal bleeding.

Your best course of action for prevention is to increase your fluid and fiber intake and to eat a lot of fiber-rich foods, such as fruits, vegetables, and whole grains. Constipation can aggravate them. Additionally, avoiding strain when you urinate and performing pelvic-floor exercises (Kegels) can be helpful.

dental wellness

Want to increase the likelihood that you will safely carry your child to term? Make sure to grab the dental floss and brush your teeth at least twice a day, as research has shown that maintaining good oral hygiene and dental health is associated with longer pregnancies.

25th week of pregnancy symptoms

Acid reflux or indigestion

Snoring

Tickled hands (carpal tunnel)

dysfunction of the symphysis pubis (SPD)

Irritable bowel syndrome (RLS)

rapid growth of hair

Advice for This Week

Do you feel down? Consult your physician.

Surprisingly frequently, women experience postpartum depression (PPD) and depression during pregnancy. Crying, agitation, a lack of appetite, and trouble sleeping are a few symptoms.

According to one study, denying happy feelings, or saying "I don't deserve to be happy," may raise your risk of developing the disorder. Sounds recognizable? Discuss getting help with your doctor as soon as you can.

Snack on nutritious candies

Need suggestions for sweet snacks? When you're experiencing a midday slump, munch on some carrot or oat bran muffins with a piece of cheese or a container of yogurt. These can take the place of donuts and coffee cake.

A smoothie, apple wedges and peanut butter, all-fruit jam spread on a whole wheat English muffin, cottage cheese with strawberries, tangerines, and cinnamon, yogurt with walnuts and dried fruit on top, or apple wedges and cottage cheese are other options for reviving yourself.

Keep track of any eye symptoms.

Another seemingly arbitrary body part that is impacted by those weird hormones is your eyes. Is that you, Honey? During this time, it's possible that your vision won't be as clear and that wearing contact lenses won't be as comfortable.

Another twist in the eye tale: Ironically, despite the fact that you're retaining fluid, your eyes might be drier than ever.

But don't worry, eye symptoms will go away after delivery just like skin symptoms did. Just make sure to inform your doctor of the situation so they can "keep an eye on things."

Streamline your shopping list.

If you want to stock up on nutritious staples, you don't have to purchase processed food.

Think small, convenient, and ready-to-nibble when choosing produce, snacks, and dairy products. Seek out single-serve yogurt containers, 8-ounce cottage cheese tubs, individually wrapped string cheese, fresh fruit salads that have already been prepared, mini packs of baby carrots, and tiny boxes or bags of raisins, nuts, dried fruit, and trail mix.

You should definitely use frozen produce, pre-washed salad bags, and quick-cooking meat and poultry as additional time-saving measures (for stir-fry or fajitas).

WEEK 26

EXPLORE WEEK 26 0f PREGNANCY

You are almost in the third trimester at 26 weeks pregnant, rounding out the second trimester.

This week, your baby's adorable eyes might open. Additionally, as your tummy grows larger, you might experience more clumsiness and pregnancy insomnia symptoms.

How has your baby's growth been this week? She is now more than 14 inches long and weighs a full 2 pounds.

There is still plenty of room for your baby to grow inside your uterus, so don't worry if it starts to feel a little crowded soon. Just that she won't have as much room to perform those somersaults, cartwheels, and other Olympic feats with your tiny gymnast.

Brainwave activity begins to occur

Check out what else is happening this week: At this point in fetal development, your baby's brain-wave activity is ramping up, which means your little one can now not only hear noises but also respond to them. Naturally, not in so many words, but rather with an increase in movement or pulse rate.

enlarged navel

Your enlarging uterus begins to swell around the middle to the end of your second trimester, pushing your abdomen forward and causing your navel to protrude like the timer on a well-done turkey even though your baby isn't quite "well done." A few months after delivery, your belly button should return to its original position, despite possibly having that stretched-out, "lived in" appearance.

Consider the positive: It gives you a chance to clean out all the lint that has accumulated there since you were a child. If your belly button piercing becomes too tight, you may need to remove it.

Insomnia

There are, however, a variety of strategies you can try that should keep you in bed instead of pacing the floor, such as daytime exercise, daily exposure to fresh air, and limiting fluids before bed.

The infant's womb movements

With all the kicking going on, do you feel like the Karate Kid? Your baby is actually practicing a variety of motions that will eventually be used in everyday life, such as pedaling against your belly, which is akin to practicing for a walk.

Fetal movements will become much more organized as your baby's nervous system matures. And those movements will get a lot stronger as she grows bigger and stronger.

She might also try extending that leg so far that the foot catches between your ribs. The next time you are attacked, try shifting positions or performing some of your own stretching. When your knee-jerker jerks just a little too hard, you can also gently push your baby back with your hand. Your little slugger might be able to be sent back into the ring's corner!

26th week of pregnancy symptoms

Gas and bloating

Obstetrical brain

Clumsiness

Migraines

distorted vision

Tips for You This Week Regarding Round Ligament Pain

After 6 o'clock in the evening, drink in moderation.

Reduce the amount of alcohol you consume after dinner (just get enough fluids) if frequent bathroom visits prevent you from getting a good night's sleep.

your meat thoroughly.

You don't want your meat, fish, or poultry to be partially baked. If the juice from a fork pierced through cooked chicken comes out red, the chicken is undercooked; return the chicken to the oven and heat it through until the juices run clear.

To check that the middle of cooked meat and chops is gray or brown with no rare spots, slice through the thickest part of the food.

And cook fish until it is thoroughly cooked rather than searing it and serving it rare or medium. Even better, use a good meat thermometer to check the temperature.

Ah, baby, let's go!

You are aware that exercising light to moderately while pregnant is healthy for you

(as long as your doctor has given the all clear). But once you begin to feel the baby kick, you might discover that you always have a little workout partner with you when you go for a walk, swim some laps, or work out in the gym.

But keep in mind that every fetus reacts to Mom's exercise regimen differently. While some may be soothed to sleep by the movement, others may appear to begin their own workout, saying, "Look, I can kickbox, too!"

Consult your doctor about the appropriate level of intensity for you and your tiny workout partner as well as the type of fetal movement you can anticipate both during and after your workout.

Maintain proper posture.

Standing up, let alone standing up straight, isn't always easy with your growing belly and your hurting back. However, try to avoid having the tendency to throw your shoulders back and thrust your hips and stomach forward as you walk because doing so could make your pregnancy pains worse.

Instead, when you're moving around, try to maintain a straight line between your shoulders and hips. To experience this, lean back against a wall. Perform some standing pelvic tilts while you're at it. Put a pillow behind your lower back for support to help you sit smartly.

Avoid raw eggs

Cook eggs until the yolks have started to thicken and the whites have solidified.

And unless you're using pasteurized eggs, never consume salad dressings, sauces, or mousse-style desserts made with raw eggs.

Avoid eating uncooked cake batter or cookie dough as well. Even though it's delicious, it's a good idea to stop even if you're not pregnant!

WEEK 27

EXPLORE WEEK 27 0f PREGNANCY

On the other hand, your infant is developing his own skills. And let's just say that he enjoys hearing your voice.

Also, don't be surprised if you start to notice small jumps in your expanding belly all of a sudden. Your child might be experiencing hiccups!

How much do I weigh at 27 weeks?

Your baby is now more than a foot long and measures around 1412 inches by the end of the second trimester. His weight, which is currently around 2 pounds, is also gradually rising. It has increased by twofold since four weeks ago.

The term "fetal position" refers to how most babies of this age, including yours, still enjoy cuddling up in a slightly curled position inside the uterus.

Emphysema and swelling

The feet, ankles, and hands in particular experience mild swelling of the extremities in nearly 3 out of 4 pregnant women, and it may get worse now.

Talk to your doctor if it seems excessive because it could be a symptom of preeclampsia. When it is, however, it is often accompanied by a number of other symptoms like high blood pressure and protein in the urine. You shouldn't be concerned if you don't have any of these symptoms.

Avoid sitting or standing for long periods of time, try pregnancy-safe exercise like walking or swimming, and sit or sleep with your feet elevated to help relieve swelling. Hey, you're the one who deserves to raise your tired feet!

Additionally, make sure you get enough water each day. Staying hydrated is more likely to reduce swelling than restricting your fluid intake. And try to see the positive side of things: Edema is a transient condition; shortly after giving birth, it will completely go away.

relieve heat rash

Heat rash appears as prickly, pimply, itchy, red patches on your skin and is brought on by a combination of an already overheated pregnant body, moisture from excessive sweating, and the friction of skin rubbing against itself or against clothing, as it tends to do when there is more skin to rub.

The crease where the lower abdomen bulge rubs against the top of the pubic area, between and beneath the breasts, and on the inner thighs are the most common locations for it.

You can reduce some of the heat in your heat rash with a cool, damp compress. . Calamine lotion can also provide momentary relief and is safe to use. Ask your doctor about the best course of action if any rash or irritation persists for more than a few days.

Week 27 of pregnancy symptoms

dizziness or faintness

bluish gums

belly itch

Irritable bowel syndrome (RLS)

painful round ligaments

This Week's Tips for a Stuffy Nose

Combat swollen eyes

Try to get as much rest as you can and drink plenty of water to flush your system because water retention and fatigue are the two main causes of bags under the eyes. Drinking more causes you to retain less water.

Still too puffy for your tastes? Here are some simple solutions: Because under-eye bags and dark circles are more noticeable in the morning, When you wake up, place something cool over your eyes. The perennially popular chilled cucumber slices, iced tea bags, chilled spoons, or a bag of frozen blueberries are all good options. If you're so inclined, concealer and mascara can also be helpful.

Select the finest salmon.

Have you heard varying salmon tales? Eat a lot of it; it's healthy for you. or "Watch your weight; eating too much is bad for you!"

Salmon is undoubtedly one of nature's best sources of DHA, an omega-3 fatty acid that is good for moms and babies and helps the brain and mood.

Try to choose organically raised farmed or wild foods, which both contain more of those healthy fats.

monitor your heart rate while exercising

It's more crucial than ever to monitor your heart rate while you exercise now that you're pumping for two.

Use the exercise talk test instead of taking your pulse to determine how much you're exerting yourself. If you can't talk and exercise at the same time, your heart rate is likely too high.

Maintain a food diary.

Try keeping a food journal and noting your meals before you experience episodes of restless leg syndrome if restless leg syndrome is making you crazy.

Keeping a journal can help you identify the foods that either make your symptoms worse or better.

Combat bloat

We are aware of your bloating and gas. It's typical! You might want to substitute less gassy vegetables like spinach and carrots for foods like broccoli and asparagus to help alleviate the issue.

Additionally, remember to drink a lot of water and choose smaller meals because the more food you eat at once, the more gas you'll eventually pass.

WEEK 28

EXPLORE WEEK 28 0f PREGNANCY

Congratulations on the beginning of the third trimester!

If you're experiencing typical week 28 symptoms like sciatica and back pain, you might not always feel like celebrating. But hopefully, now that you're in your seventh month of pregnancy, you're still fairly at ease.

Baby can now blink and even dream as they become more and more skilled every day. And that's just the start.

Your tiny unfinished project currently weighs around 214 pounds and measures almost 15 inches from head to toe.

Dreaming of your child at 28 weeks' gestation? Perhaps your infant is also dreaming of you. A growing fetus's brain wave activity reveals various sleep cycles, including the rapid eye movement phase, which is when dreams take place.

Sciatica (tingling leg pain)

If you ever thought that pregnancy was "comfortable," those days are most likely long gone. Your feet may be swollen, you may be getting tired all over again, and your backache is a pain that just won't go away. Now, your baby's kicking (or lack thereof) keeps you up at night and worried during the day.

It might seem like your baby is literally getting on your nerves even though she hasn't yet started crying. Your child's head and your expanding uterus may rest on the sciatic nerve in the lower part of your spine as she positions herself for delivery.

If that occurs, you might experience sciatica, which is a sharp, shooting pain, tingling, or numbness that begins in your buttocks and radiates down the back of your legs. Sciatica pain can occasionally be quite severe, and while it may subside if your baby shifts positions, it can also last until you give birth.

The discomfort can be relieved with a heating pad, a warm bath, stretches, or even some self-imposed bed rest. Some complementary and alternative therapies can also be used.

Do you have sensitive skin?

Even in people who have never had sensitive skin before, it can become sensitive during pregnancy.

Some body parts may react as a result of being dry and flaky, while others may do so as a result of heat rash or an outside irritant, such as the lotion you've been using for the past ten years but which is now giving you the willies.

The belly is usually the most delicate area because of how much it stretches. Your hips and thighs are two additional potential trouble areas.

A small amount of calamine lotion should relieve itchy areas. Ask your doctor about the best course of action if any rash or irritation persists for more than a few days. Avoid products that contain a ton of additives, dyes, or fragrances as any of these can make the situation worse.

28th week of pregnancy symptoms

Gas and bloating

dizziness or faintness

dysfunction of the symphysis pubis (SPD)

clogged nose

bluish gums

Pregnancy mask (melasma) advice for this week

Have the circumcision discussion

You might not have given the decision of whether or not to circumcise a boy baby much thought prior to becoming pregnant. But if you're expecting a son, you'll have to make a choice, and it might be challenging if you don't have any religious or cultural traditions to help you.

It might be a good idea to consider this now if you're expecting a boy. Get your child's pediatrician's perspective as well!

determine your Rhe status

Are you aware of your Rh status—whether positive or negative? If not, it's critical to ascertain.

The majority of people's red blood cells contain a protein called Rh factor. Rh positivity is the presence of it; Rh negativity is the absence of it.

Your status typically doesn't matter much unless you're pregnant, but issues could arise if, for instance, you're Rh negative and your child is Rh positive.

Your immune system may identify your baby's blood cells as "foreign" substances in the case of Rh incompatibility and mobilize a horde of antibodies to attack them.

Rh-immune globulin, also known as RhoGAM, will need to be injected into you this week if you are Rh negative and your child is Rh positive in order to prevent the formation of antibodies.

Up the ante

Eat iron-rich foods like chicken, beans, spinach, tofu, beef, and enriched cereals during the third trimester as this is when babies absorb the majority of their iron stores.

Vitamin C is iron's best friend besides Popeye because it can increase iron absorption. So while pregnant, drink some orange juice with your iron supplement, eat some red pepper with your shrimp, or mix some fresh strawberries into your oat bran cereal.

Leave out fish oil supplements.

Have you heard that taking fish oil supplements is the simplest way to get your DHA, particularly if you don't like fatty fish? While they may be simple to swallow, they are not always simple to keep down when you are pregnant.

Let's face it, you burp enough as it is; if you don't want to be doing it all day, take fish oil— choose a prenatal vitamin that contains DHA already, or if that has the same effect, you might want to try a vegetarian DHA flaxseed supplement, which is typically easier on the aftertaste. Before including any supplement in your daily routine, consult your doctor first.

selecting a birthing class

A good time to look into childbirth classes is right now. Choose a course at the hospital or one taught by a local teacher, but register early so you can finish well in advance of the due date. Inquire as to whether your program includes instruction in breastfeeding, CPR, and baby care (it should).

have unique specifications? For those with experience who need to review their techniques, there are classes available. classes for mothers trying to have a vaginal birth after a c-section (VBAC), as well as classes for those who are expecting multiples. Virtual classes are now available everywhere else.

Whichever class you enroll in, check to see if the instructor has a national certification in childbirth education. As an added bonus: Be sure to submit your bill because your insurance provider might reimburse you for your tuition.

Plan a visit to the hospital

Inquire with your doctor about when and how to set one up. It's a great way to get a feel for the area and makes it easier to picture where the magic will take place!

WEEK 29

EXPLORE WEEK 29 0f PREGNANCY

By week 29 of pregnancy, if you haven't already, you should begin performing daily kick counts once or twice a day (or more).

Although there isn't much room left for the baby, you should still be able to feel him moving around frequently. Be sure to contact your practitioner if you notice any variations in frequency.

In terms of symptoms, you might notice varicose veins and your nails might be growing more quickly than usual.

Added hiccups

Your young child is still hiccupping. They don't bother the baby and feel to you like gentle, rhythmic taps.

Close quarters

Your womb is getting a little congested as your little bean bulks up, so the hard kicks you were feeling will now feel more like jabs and pokes.

Your baby is currently 1512 to 16 inches long and weighs 2 12 to 3 pounds at 29 weeks of pregnancy. He still has some weight gain to do even though he is getting very close to reaching his birth length.

In fact, he'll nearly triple his weight over the course of the next 11 weeks, more than doubling it.

baby kicking count

You'll mostly feel elbows and knees jabbing and poking you because there isn't much room in your baby's new home.

Your baby is stronger and more enthusiastically responding to all kinds of stimuli, including movement, sounds, light, and that candy bar you ate 30 minutes ago, so they will be more vigorous and less erratic than before.

According to your doctor's advice, this means it's a good idea to start doing a kick count once or twice a day. It's also a good justification for a break.

dilated veins

If you're like the 20% of expectant mothers who develop varicose veins, you might start noticing some new additions to your skin by week 29 of pregnancy.

When you're expecting, these swollen blood vessels may develop or worsen, though they're rarely a cause for alarm. They appear because of an increase in blood volume, pressure from the expanding uterus on the pelvic veins, and vein relaxation brought on by hormones during pregnancy.

Varicose veins can be painful for some pregnant women, but not for others.

Your best bet is to keep your circulation moving by avoiding standing or sitting for extended periods of time if you want to prevent or minimize their appearance. Try to exercise every day and consider putting on specialized support hose, which can be beneficial. After delivery, varicose veins typically disappear within a few months.

Performing a kick count

Get into the habit of counting kicks once or twice a day, depending on what your doctor advises, to make sure everything is fine inside. It's best to do it lying down because babies tend to wake up when their mothers are sleeping, a pattern that usually continues after birth, or sitting if lying on your back is uncomfortable for you.

Count every movement, including swishes and rolls, until you reach 10. Have a small snack and try again if you haven't reached 10 in an hour; that blood sugar rush will probably get baby back on the move. If you haven't reached 10 in an hour, your little Rockette may just be taking a break right now.

Just keep in mind that less than 10 movements in a period of two hours require a call to your doctor. Despite the likelihood that everything is fine, it is always preferable to be safe than sorry.

29th week of pregnancy symptoms

Constipation

Migraines

Hemorrhoids

Baby brain Rapidly expanding nails

Acid reflux or indigestion

Advice for This Week

Purchase breast pads

Buy lots of nursing pads right away! Before the birth of your child, your breasts may begin to secrete colostrum, a thin, yellowish fluid that serves as the baby's first food if you choose to breastfeed.

Colostrum is easier for the newborn to digest in the first few days after birth because it has more protein but less fat and sugar than more developed breast milk.

Maintain movement to avoid RLS

You already struggle to get a good night's sleep due to pregnancy insomnia, leg cramps, heartburn, and the urgent need to use the restroom every two hours. And now that you're in your third trimester, restless legs syndrome—yet another pregnancy symptom—is keeping you up all night (RLS).

RLS is frequent in the third trimester for unknown reasons. Make sure you consume enough iron and move around enough throughout the day.

Decorate the baby room on a tight budget.

It's a lot of fun to set up the nursery for your child. Not so much when you look at the price tags on the gliders, changing tables, and cribs. Use a few DIY decorations for the remainder of the nursery if you've already spent all of your money on the major purchases.

Hang some old photographs, cheap online prints, or older siblings' drawings on the walls, or get crafty with stencils and decals. Or arrange some vibrant toys on the open shelves to make eye-catching displays.

Use the proper fitness equipment.

It's crucial to have the proper equipment when working out during pregnancy because your body is more susceptible to fatigue and overheating and your sense of balance is impaired.

Make sure you have supportive, comfortable shoes, a top-notch sports bra, water to drink before, during, and after working out, a cool, wet cloth in a small plastic bag to wipe your face or neck, and just in case, a phone, some cash, and some identification.

Think about cord blood banking.

A definition first After delivery, cord blood is what is still present in the placenta and umbilical cord. What makes this blood so crucial? This is so that certain diseases, like some types of cancer, can be treated using stem cells found in cord blood.

Just after the baby is born, a doctor or hospital employee will take blood from the umbilical cord vein. The procedure lasts about five minutes and is painless.

Understand contractions

In other words, if you've already experienced Braxton Hicks contractions, you might experience them a little more frequently than usual.

To understand what to expect when you experience contractions, ask your doctor how to distinguish between Braxton Hicks, or "rehearsal" contractions, and actual labor contractions.

WEEK 30

EXPLORE WEEK30 0f PREGNANCY

At 30 weeks pregnant, your baby is growing quickly, which means your bump may be expanding even more. The baby's rapidly growing brain accounts for a sizable portion of that growth.

At the same time, you might be welcoming back a few of the early pregnancy symptoms, like frequent urination, that you thought you had waved goodbye to at the end of the first trimester.

Your expanding belly is a definite indicator that your baby is growing every day; she currently weighs about 3 pounds. Over the next seven weeks, she will gain weight at a rate of about half a pound per week.

Lanugo is vanishing.

The lanugo, that soft, downy hair covering your baby's body, is starting to disappear now that the brain and new fat cells in the baby's body are controlling body temperature.

That fur coat is no longer required! But when your baby is born, you might notice a few stray hairs on her back and shoulders.

They've returned!

There are just 10 weeks left in your pregnancy. Many of the early pregnancy symptoms you thought you'd outgrown, such as the constant urge to urinate because your baby's head is pressing against your bladder, tender breasts that are preparing to produce milk, fatigue, and pregnancy heartburn, may be returning to haunt you, at least in part.

Or you might be one of the fortunate ones who still feels pretty good; just keep in mind that everything is normal and that everyone is unique!

Heartburn

You might experience the sensation of having a flamethrower in your chest these days. One of the most typical (and annoying) side effects of pregnancy is indigestion.

This is why: The ring of muscle that separates the esophagus from the stomach is also relaxed by pregnancy hormones, which are also responsible for relaxing your pelvic muscles so you can deliver your baby.

The outcome: The infernal inferno results from food and digestive fluids traveling upstream from your stomach into your chest and throat. Your stomach is now being compressed by your expanding uterus, which only adds fuel to the fire.

Then how do you pronounce relief? Avoid foods that can upset your stomach, such as spicy, fatty, or fried foods, chocolate, and tomato sauce, among other things. eat smaller meals and avoid lying down immediately after or while snacking. Maintain a supply of Tums or Rolaids nearby as well, as they provide a beneficial calcium bonus.

Fortunately, heartburn will disappear once your baby is born, at least until you try to eat dinner in the middle of a colic marathon.

Week 30 of pregnancy symptoms

Modifications in fetal movement

Gas and bloating

enlarged ankles and feet

Constipation

Stretch stains

Tips for Overcoming Fatigue This Week

Pillows for support

Breathless? Your diaphragm is being squeezed by your growing baby. Even light physical exertion may cause you to feel dizzy as your pregnancy progresses.

While standing up straight can give your lungs a little breathing room, it won't completely alleviate breathlessness during pregnancy. Try lying on your left side with pillows supporting you while you sleep at night.

Select flats.

Put your heels away! You become clumsier than usual due to your altered sense of gravity and loosening joints (caused by the vital hormone relaxin). By wearing flats and paying attention to your steps, prevent falls.

Consult your doctor about having an episiotomy during labor. Right before delivery, a surgical cut is made in your perineum, the muscle between your vagina and your anus, to increase the size of your baby's exit.

Episiotomies were commonplace in the past, but nowadays they are rarely performed unless there is a valid reason. What you want to hear is, "I only perform them if absolutely necessary," from your doctor.

Keep your Kegels in mind

Kegel exercises may sound silly, at least when spoken aloud, but they are effective at strengthening the pelvic floor.

Why? A stronger pelvic floor can help with pregnancy and postpartum symptoms like hemorrhoids and urinary incontinence by better supporting your uterus, bladder, and bowels. More good news: Kegel exercises are simple to perform anywhere.

To use them, contract the muscles in the area around your vagina and your bottom and hold for as long as it takes to stop the urine from flowing. Then slowly let go and do it again. Try to complete three sets of 20 per day. Try performing them while having sex.

Reduce the retention of water

Contrary to popular belief, excessive water retention and swelling can be controlled by consuming plenty of liquids.

Keeping the fluids flowing (along with reducing your salt intake) can prevent too many from accumulating where you'd rather they didn't, even though some pregnancy edema is to be expected when you're expecting and represents a normal and necessary increase in body fluids.

WEEK 31

EXPLORE WEEK 31 0f PREGNANCY

Your baby is more active than ever inside his developing brain at this stage of pregnancy—31 weeks—pedaling with his feet, sucking his thumb, and honing other critical life skills.

You might be using the restroom more often and getting tired more quickly these days.

Your baby is already over three pounds in weight and is close to reaching his full birth length, but he still needs to gain another three to five pounds before the big day.

The brain of your newborn is currently growing more quickly than ever and working overtime. He must create billions of connections between individual nerve cells, and they are forming very quickly. He is currently analyzing data, observing light, and picking up signals from all five senses.

Your baby may not be able to smell very much at this time, but he or she can probably taste and smell the various foods you consume through the amniotic fluid, as well as get a whiff of some of the cosmetics you use (which also wind up in the amniotic fluid).

Fortunately for you and your baby, his first scent will be yours, which will quickly become one of his favorites.

Breathlessness At 31 weeks pregnant, you can now feel your uterus 4 inches above your belly button. This indicates that your uterus is relocating all of your internal organs, which will put more pressure on your diaphragm and lungs, making it more difficult for them to expand fully.

The outcome: Until your baby drops near the end of pregnancy to prepare for birth, your body will be spare on air. Although you may find this shortness of breath to be extremely uncomfortable, your baby is content as can be because the placenta is providing him with oxygen.

When your baby descends into your pelvis in preparation for delivery toward the end of your pregnancy, you might experience less difficulty breathing. Until then, make sure to eat smaller, more frequent meals, sleep propped up on your left side so that your lungs have more room to... well, breathe, and stand as straight as you can given the weight you're carrying around.

How a child reacts to sex

Both of these reactions are entirely normal and in no way suggest that your baby is aware of what is happening; rather, they simply show that he is enjoying the ride.

pregnancy symptoms

increased urination

Backaches

Clumsiness

Obstetrical brain

issues with sleep

Periodic headaches

Advice for This Week

swerve bumpers

Observe any facial swelling

It might not just be prenatal weight. Consult your doctor if you notice a sudden increase in facial swelling.

Preeclampsia is a condition that typically manifests after week 20, along with headaches, changes in vision, and swelling. It is characterized by an abrupt onset of high blood pressure, severe facial and hand swelling, and symptoms that suggest certain organs may not be functioning properly, such as protein in the urine.

Select supportive footwear.

Get yourself to a shoe store, but go when your feet are at their puffiest, late in the day. Get a pair of elasticized slippers while you're at it and wear them whenever you can get away with it. Additionally, keep a pair of flip-flops on hand in case you experience postpartum swelling of the feet and ankles as the pregnancy fluids leave your body after giving birth.

Avoid having varicose veins

Varicose veins, or swollen blood vessels, are typically painless and harmless, despite the fact that we know you don't like them.

Because you have more blood pumping through your body and your expanding uterus is pressing against pelvic veins, more blood is able to pool in your legs during pregnancy, which causes them to develop or become more pronounced. Hormones only make things worse by relaxing blood vessels.

Perform easy stretches.

One method to unwind your mind and relax your muscles is to: Do this simple stretch whenever you want, anywhere. Start by cocking your head to one side while attempting to melt your shoulders down your back rather than raising them. Exhale after three seconds of holding. On the opposite side, repeat.

Do this several times per day, whether at your desk, while you're in line at the doctor's office or at the grocery store.

WEEK 32

EXPLORE WEEK32 0f PREGNANCY

Your infant is working on practical skills like breathing, swallowing, and sucking.

And in preparation for the big day, you might be performing some of your own rehearsals through Braxton Hicks (or practice) contractions.

How much does my baby weigh at 32 weeks?

How is your baby doing? She weighs between 3 and 4 pounds and grows to a maximum height of 15 to 17 inches as she begins to prepare for her big debut.

Head down or breech for the fetus?

Instead of your baby's characteristic rocking and rolling at 32 weeks pregnant, you probably feel tapping and wriggling. That's because your baby is currently curled up again, making it difficult for her to move around in a comfortable but efficient manner (you try standing up in those cramped quarters!).

Your baby will likely begin to settle into the head-down, bottoms-up presentation in your pelvis between 32 and 38 weeks of pregnancy in order to prepare for delivery. It's easier to deliver a baby who comes out head first because the fetus' head fits better at the bottom of your inverted, pear-shaped uterus.

Don't worry if your baby hasn't assumed the head-down position just yet. Less than 5% of babies prefer the bottom-down (or breech) position by full-term. Even in the restricted space of your uterus, she still has a good chance of flipping before giving birth.

Baby's sleeping patterns

In relation to the big day, I hope you're getting enough rest because your child undoubtedly is. Your baby is sleeping like a baby, with regular sleep and wake cycles, in anticipation of your first date.

contractions of Braxton Hicks

They last between 15 and 30 seconds, though they occasionally go as long as two minutes, and feel like a tightening that starts at the top of your uterus and moves downward.

How can you tell they aren't actually working? Try getting up if you're lying down or walking if you've been sitting because they will stop if you change positions. If they are actual labor contractions, they will get stronger and more frequent over time.

So if your child hasn't yet positioned themselves head-down, don't worry. Even in the restricted space of your uterus, she still has a good chance of flipping before giving birth.

Baby's sleeping patterns

In relation to the big day, I hope you're getting enough rest because your child undoubtedly is. Your baby is sleeping like a baby, with regular sleep and wake cycles, in anticipation of your first date.

contractions of Braxton Hicks

They last between 15 and 30 seconds, though they occasionally go as long as two minutes, and feel like a tightening that starts at the top of your uterus and moves downward.

How can you tell they aren't actually working? Try getting up if you're lying down or walking if you've been sitting because they will stop if you change positions. Call your doctor if you think they are labor contractions because they will get stronger and more frequent if they are. Try taking a warm bath to ease the discomfort in the interim when they're just practice ones.

pregnancy symptoms

Constipation

Leg twitches

dizziness or faintness

Hemorrhoids

Colostrum (leaky breasts)

stomach and skin itch

Advice for This Week

Make a list of your dreams.

Maintain a dream journal! These days, thanks to pregnancy hormones, your night visions might be especially surreal.

During the third trimester of pregnancy, when sleep is more erratic and you may start to daydream more frequently, pregnancy dreams and daydreams usually reach their peak.

discover early labor symptoms

You might be wondering how you'll know your labor symptoms are the real deal if you haven't experienced labor before.

In case it's not obvious, familiarize yourself with the symptoms of labor, which include regular, closer-spaced contractions, period-like cramps, vaginal bleeding or spotting, a persistent dull backache, diarrhea, and a tightening sensation in the uterus. Though don't count on it, your water might even break before you arrive at the hospital!

Take a snack.

You might notice that your appetite is waning right now — shocking! Your large uterus is cramping up inside of you. Instead of eating large meals, try to eat regular, small snacks like a bite of a banana with almond butter or hummus and whole wheat crackers.

Frequently moisturize

Feeling a little crocodile-like? Dry, itchy skin is another side effect of your growing body, along with that belly that just keeps growing.

Here is a helpful calming technique: Early in the day, moisturize. In order to trap moisture in, apply moisturizers while your skin is still damp because your skin is still particularly sensitive these days.

Utilize pelvic tilts

Treating your pelvis well will ensure a pain-free pregnancy and delivery. Regularly performing pelvic tilts is one method for strengthening your pelvis. These quick, portable exercises can ease backaches during pregnancy and labor, strengthen your abs, and facilitate a smoother delivery.

Tilts should be performed while standing now that you are in your third trimester, so locate the closest wall. Stand up straight and relax your spine to perform a standing pelvic tilt. Put your small of your back against the wall while taking a deep breath. After about five minutes, breathe out before repeating.

WEEK 33

EXPLORE WEEK33 0f PREGNANCY

You're approaching the middle of the third trimester now that you're 33 weeks along.

Your baby has reached the length he'll be at birth, but he's still gaining about half a pound per week.

Because of the crowding around your lungs, you may notice this rapid growth in the form of sharper kicks and shortness of breath.

At 33 weeks, how big is my baby?

This week, your baby could be anywhere between 16 and 17 inches long and could grow another full inch — especially if he's been on the short side.

He weighs over 414 pounds and continues to gain weight at a rate of about half a pound per week. Before the big debut, weight gain can range from a third to a full doubling.

With that much baby inside your uterus, your amniotic fluid level has likely peaked at 33 weeks, implying that you now have more baby than fluid. That's why some of his pokes and kicks feel so sharp these days.

If your uterus had eyes, you'd notice your fetus acting more and more like a baby, with his eyes closing during sleep and opening during wakefulness.

Because the uterine walls are becoming thinner, more light enters the womb, allowing your baby to distinguish between day and night. If only baby could remember the distinction on the outside!

Insomnia

Your body needs rest at 33 weeks pregnant, so remember that worrying about it won't help, nor will staring at the clock as the minutes tick by.

nstead, make an effort to relax before and after going to bed. Before going to bed, take a warm bath and possibly a warm cup of milk, and avoid exercising, screen time, eating, or drinking too close to bedtime. You could also request a massage from your partner. You've earned it!

If you can't sleep, read a book or listen to soothing music until you fall asleep. And, on the bright side, pregnancy insomnia is excellent preparation for future sleepless nights!

Omega-3 essential fatty acids

According to research, infants born to mothers whose diets are high in omega-3 fatty acids (DHA), which are mostly found in fish oils, have an advantage in terms of early development.

pregnancy symptoms

Fetal movement is very strong.

Veins that are varicose

Round ligament discomfort

Nail modifications

Clumsiness and shortness of breath

Pregnancy mind

Braxton Contractions caused by Hicks

This Week's Suggestions

Increase your calcium intake.

If milk gives you a sour taste, there are plenty of other ways to get your calcium. Blend milk into smoothies or soups, or skip it entirely and get your calcium from other dairy products.

One cup of yogurt contains the same amount of calcium as one cup of milk, and an ounce of cheese, as well as a quarter-cup of grated cheese, also provide a serving.

You can also get your calcium fix from fortified fruit juice, such as orange, grapefruit, apple, and cranberry juice, as well as calcium-enriched soy milk and cheese.

Remember that skipping milk means missing out on not only calcium but also vitamin D. Yogurt and cheese may be high in the former but low in the latter.

Because your body produces vitamin D in response to sunlight, getting enough of it is as simple as spending a few minutes in the sun each day. Check to see if your prenatal tablet contains the sunshine vitamin. If you drink soy milk, look for one that is vitamin D-enriched.

Change to lighter weights.

Lifting heavy weights raises blood pressure in your body, causing you to hold your breath and potentially impairing blood flow to the uterus. Furthermore, loosened ligaments may result in injury.

Switch to lighter weights and do more reps — or simply avoid weights until after delivery.

Write a letter to your child.

You have a lot of hopes and dreams for your child, and each one is worth remembering and sharing. Write a letter — or series of letters — to your baby to record them before you forget.

Do you find it strange to write to a fetus? Simply speak from the heart. Discuss what this pregnancy means to you and how it is affecting your body and your life. Recall the foods you craved, how you finally decided on a name for your baby, and the colors you chose for the nursery.

Share your feelings about finding out you were pregnant, feeling those first kicks, and learning your baby's gender (if you have). Consider what you might do together in the future. Do you envision yourself pushing a swing in the park or throwing a football on your front lawn? Consider what your child's future might be like.

Your letter to your baby will undoubtedly become one of your most prized possessions — and, eventually, one of your child's.

Prevent stomach upset

If your body has difficulty digesting lactose (a type of sugar), drinking milk may cause cramps, gas, bloating, and diarrhea.

You could buy lactose-free milk or take a lactase capsule before drinking it, but there are other ways to increase your calcium intake while avoiding stomach upset.

One option: Consume naturally aged hard cheeses such as cheddar, Parmesan, and Swiss (they lose more than half their lactose during processing). Active yogurt cultures, on the other hand, contain good bacteria that break down lactose.

You can also reduce the amount of milk you consume. It's possible that your stomach can handle smaller portions, such as a half-cup at a time. Alternatively, a thin slice of mozzarella.

Finally, because lactose is easier to digest when combined with other foods, especially those high in fiber, drink your milk with whole grain cereal or spread that cheese on a slice of whole wheat bread.

Sleep on your left side.

You haven't been able to sleep on your back — or your stomach — in a few months, but now that you're officially a side sleeper, consider rolling onto your left side at night (though either side works).

Why? According to some experts, sleeping on your left side is the best sleeping position for both you and your baby because it allows for maximum blood flow and nutrients to the placenta. It may also help to alleviate swelling in your feet and ankles.

WEEK 34

EXPLORE WEEK34 0f PREGNANCY

You're 34 weeks pregnant and in month 8 of your pregnancy.

Your baby is now about 5 pounds, which is the same as a standard bag of flour.

Meanwhile, your uterus continues to grow (and grow) in order to accommodate the larger bun in the oven.

At 34 weeks, how big is my baby?

This week, your baby weighs 514 pounds and could grow to be 18 inches long. Do you require a visual? Hold a 5-pound bag of flour in your arms like it's your soon-to-be-born baby; cradle it, and you'll get strange looks in the baking aisle.

Vision shifts

But wait...are you hallucinating? You're probably not seeing as well as you used to. That's because your eyes are yet another part of your body that can be affected

by those pesky pregnancy hormones, which are also wreaking havoc on your digestive tract and ligaments.

These days, not only can your vision appear blurry, but a decrease in tear production can leave your eyes dry and irritated, especially if you wear contact lenses.

Furthermore, an increase in fluid behind your eyes' lenses can cause them to change shape temporarily, making some women more nearsighted or farsighted than usual. Wearing glasses rather than contact lenses may be more comfortable for you. week 34

Gas and bloating

Constipation

Vaginal discharge has increased.

Hemorrhoids

Backaches

Cramps in the legs

Marks from stretching

Edema (swelling in feet and ankles)

Hair that grows quickly

Breathing difficulty

Insomnia

This Week's Tips for Leaking Colostrum

Set up the car seat

Have you installed the car seat you purchased? A better question would be, "Did you install it correctly?" Between 85 and 95 percent of new parents make mistakes.

Whatever vehicle or car seat you have, you must always follow three important rules when installing an infant car seat:

1. Your baby should always ride in the backseat, ideally in the middle seat and away from the passenger-side airbags.

2. Turn it around. Parents are advised to keep children in the rear-facing position until they reach the maximum weight or height permitted by their car seat, according to experts from the American Academy of Pediatrics (AAP) and the National Highway Traffic Safety Administration (NHTSA).

3. Ensure that the base is firmly fastened. A car seat must not swivel, slide, or tip over. Get yours checked by a qualified technician if you're unsure of how you installed it. You might be able to get your work free of charge checked by your neighborhood police or fire station.

Keep your eyes safe

Keep your sunglasses and lubricating eye drops, also referred to as "artificial tears," close at hand because your eyes may be feeling more sensitive and dry than usual.

Many are safe to use while pregnant, but first seek your doctor's advice. Soon enough, tears of joy will stream from your eyes.

For prenatal blues, seek help.

Feeling down? Between 10 and 15 percent of expectant mothers experience depression. It also makes sense why they are more likely to experience depression when they are expecting: Their emotional state can suffer from spiking hormones, stress, anxiety, and social pressure to feel a certain way.

Salt your food, but don't overdo it.

A moderate amount of salt, such as iodized table salt added to meals and lightly salted foods, actually aids your body in controlling fluid balance. Furthermore, drastically reducing sodium intake is bad for the developing baby.

However, bear in mind that too much salt is unhealthy for anyone, pregnant or not, and can even make you puff more, so don't finish the pickle jar just yet.

Talk about your labor strategy.

Be sure to discuss what to do if you believe you are in labor with your doctor. It will be beneficial to receive precise instructions regarding when to contact your practitioner about contractions, what to do if your water breaks, and when, how, and if.

WEEK 35

EXPLORE WEEK35 0f PREGNANCY

You're finishing up month 8 of your pregnancy at 35 weeks, leaving just one more month.

By lowering his or her head, your child may be beginning to formulate an escape strategy while making other crucial preparations like increasing body fat and brain tissue.

Your body is likewise preparing: As your uterine muscles prepare for the big day, you might experience some Braxton Hicks contractions.

How much does my baby weigh at 35 weeks?

This week, your infant is about 18 inches tall. However, at about 514 pounds, he is still gaining weight steadily. Until delivery day, he will gain anywhere from one to several pounds, along with a significant amount of baby fat.

sheet of hints

Did you know that the number of weeks of pregnancy is roughly equivalent to the distance in centimeters from the top of your pubic bone to the top of your uterus?

Therefore, your doctor will probably use a tape measure to measure about 35 centimeters when you are 35 weeks pregnant. It's a simple way to keep track of how far along you are, not that you'd ever forget.

selecting a doula

Describe a doula. The phrase "woman's servant" is translated literally. If only you could locate a cook, massage therapist, and chauffeur right now...

When you need help the most, a doula can serve as a double agent. The birth doula is a friend who has received professional training to offer support and a hand to hold during labor.

Periodic headaches

dilated veins

Hemorrhoids

bluish gums

A skin rash

a worsening clumsiness

Obstetrical brain

Braxton contractions of Hicks

Advice for This Week

Do some pain research.

There are many safe and efficient medical options available today that can reduce some of the labor involved in giving birth. It is possible to plan your birth so that you experience little to no pain, are awake throughout the entire procedure, and can welcome your baby as he or she is born.

Make sure you are aware of all your options for reducing labor pain, such as breathing exercises and local anesthesia. As the time draws closer, you might have second thoughts about certain details. Buy plenty of nasal strips

The pregnancy hormones progesterone and estrogen can swell the mucous membranes in your nose, giving you a stuffy nose and a pregnancy headache. (It's no surprise that this symptom is referred to as pregnancy rhinitis.)

Purchase a box of nasal strips that expand your nostrils to help with congestion. Put a small amount of petroleum jelly in each nostril if your nose is especially dry.

Establish a birth plan.

You've done all you can to prepare for labor and delivery, you've read as much as you can about pregnancy and childbirth, and you're pretty sure you know exactly how you want to have your baby, from the first contraction to the last push. A birth plan can help with that. A birth plan is, as the name implies, a written document that outlines your preferences for what happens before, during, and after labor and delivery. The best course of action, after all, is to have a plan, so begin formulating your goals for the experience right away. Be flexible, don't forget.

Continue to use the gym.

How about that as a payoff? Babies of expectant exercisers typically sleep through the night earlier, are less likely to experience colic, and have improved self-soothing skills.

Scientists believe that the beneficial relationship results from babies being stimulated during workouts in the womb through changes in heart rate and oxygen levels as well as sounds and vibrations. But who is interested in science? Let's lace up the sneakers!

Keep an eye out for hidden sugar sources.

Though some of the sugar in fruit-filled yogurts is naturally occurring sugar from the fruit and milk, contrary to what you might believe, many fruit-filled yogurts have almost as much sugar as a small candy bar.

Look for yogurts with less than 20 grams of sugar per serving, if at all possible (as low as 10 to 12 grams).

WEEK 36

EXPLORE WEEK36 0f PREGNANCY

Welcome to pregnancy week 36, which marks the beginning of the ninth month.

Due to his improved hearing, your unborn child is now more eavesdropping on conversations and may also be moving lower into your pelvis.

As hormones that loosen and soften joints begin to take effect before labor, this last month may bring more joint flexibility (and, less ideal, pelvic pain).

pregnant women waddle or walk

You've entered the last month of your pregnancy. Since your body may be feeling pretty "done" by this point, it's a good thing that your baby is almost finished cooking.

For starters, by 36 weeks pregnant, you're already walking like a penguin, a common third trimester move for expectant mothers. This new walk is real and not just in your head; Your connective tissue contains it, and those hormones are leasing and softening it.

And now that you're getting close to giving birth, that's especially crucial. It's a good thing that your pelvic bones are more flexible at this point because your baby, who has grown quite large by this point, needs to fit through them. It's your body's way of preparing to cram a large baby into a tiny space.

Pelvic pain

In addition to the fact that you now resemble your feathered friends, the drawback of all this joint flexibility is pelvic pain. It's no surprise that walking is difficult these days when you consider the weight of your heavier uterus, the pressure from your baby's head sinking deeper and deeper into your pelvis, and other factors.

Get a prenatal massage from a licensed theraplst, lie down with your hips elevated, perform some pelvic exercises, take warm baths, apply warm compresses, or try some complementary and alternative therapies to ease your discomfort. Also helpful might be a belly sling.

Baby falls ("lightening")

Believe it or not, there is a positive outcome. Remember that not all babies drop before labor starts. As your baby enters your pelvic cavity, the uterus's upward pressure on your diaphragm is released.

You'll be able to take larger, deeper breaths once this "lightening," as it's known in the pregnancy industry, occurs. Additionally, your stomach won't be as cramped, which will make eating a substantial meal more comfortable.

36th week of pregnancy symptoms

Modifications in fetal movement
Acid reflux or indigestion
Gas and bloating
Constipation
increased urination
Vaginal discharge with blood striations
belly itch
Edema (swelling in feet and ankles)
Insomnia
This Week's Nesting Instinct Advice for You

Take note of any variations in movement.

If your baby starts to squirm instead of kick or jab sharply, don't panic. There is less room for calisthenics for your cutie now.

Though you should still monitor your baby's movements every day, if you're concerned, try consuming a sweet beverage or snack and then watch to see if your baby cheers up. If there is a change in the frequency of fetal movements or a strange change in the pattern of the baby's movements, be sure to call your doctor.

Understand your mucus plug

You should be ready to lose your mucus plug, which will appear as a thick, yellow discharge that has blood in it. Before labor starts, it may occur weeks, days, or even hours.

It may still be a few weeks before labor actually begins, so there's no need to worry if your mucus plug pops out before your due date.

And even after you unplug, your baby is still secure. The fact that your body still produces cervical mucus to ward off infection means that the baby is still tightly sealed off. So you're free to engage in sexual activity, take a bath, and conduct your regular business.

Obtain a lot of B6

Ensure you have enough pyridoxine to chase your protein. Not familiar with it? It's a vitamin called B6, and its purpose is to assist your body and that of your unborn child in using all that protein for cell growth.

Consider it like this: B6 is the mortar if protein is the brick. And B6 is particularly important for the brain and nervous system development of infants.

B6 can be found in prenatal vitamins as well as foods like meat, potatoes, tomatoes, spinach, bananas, avocados, wheat germ, brown rice, wheat bran, soybeans, and oatmeal. You can see that your protein sources overlap, which makes your job even simpler.

study the phases of labor

Early, active, and transitional phases of labor are all distinct. Typically, the first of these stages lasts the longest. Fortunately, it's also the least demanding. It frequently lasts for a few hours to several weeks without any obvious or uncomfortable contractions.

Active labor, also known as the second stage, typically lasts a few hours. Your contractions will probably be stronger and longer by this point, and you'll probably be in a hospital or birthing facility (lasting about 40 to 60 seconds).

Transitional labor, the third and final stage, is frequently the most demanding one. Additionally, it is the shortest, typically lasting between 15 and an hour.

Get ready for the strep test

The Centers for Disease Control and Prevention (CDC) estimates that 1 in 4 pregnant women carry the GBS bacteria, which is typically harmless to adults. However, the GBS bacteria can seriously infect a newborn during childbirth.

Your doctor will take swabs from your rectum and vagina to test for GBS. If the test is positive, you will receive antibiotics intravenously while giving birth, greatly reducing the possibility that you will infect your unborn child.

EXPLORE WEEK37 0f PREGNANCY

You are nine months along with the end in sight at 37 weeks.

This week, your baby is honing in on some unique abilities that he'll display when he arrives (like sucking his thumb and grasping).

Your doctor will probably examine your cervix to look for signs of how you're developing at your subsequent prenatal appointment.

How much does my baby weigh at 37 weeks?

Your baby is still growing at a rate of half an ounce per day, or one pound every seven days, at 37 weeks of pregnancy. In fact, he is considered to be "early term" up until the end of week 38. The average fetus weighs about 6 pounds at this stage of development, though boys are most likely to be heavier at birth than girls.

enlargement and obliteration

When your baby decides to arrive, nobody can predict whether he will be socially early, formally late, or exactly on time. — But that doesn't stop your doctor from speculating about the start of labor.

What specifically is your doctor seeking? First, check your dilation, or the extent of your cervix's opening. Your cervix must specifically open to a 10 centimeter opening for the baby to enter the birth canal.

Your doctor will also check the cervical ripeness, also known as the cervix's consistency. It initially feels firm like the tip of your nose before softening to resemble the inside of your cheek just before giving birth.

Your doctor will then assess your cervix's effacement, or how thin it is; it will be completely thin before you deliver your baby.

Your cervix's position, which shifts from the back to the front as labor develops, will also be evaluated. The position of the baby in relation to your pelvis will also be measured by your doctor or midwife. You are nearer to giving birth the lower down your baby is.

Even though everything sounds very scientific, it's not. In some women, these processes can happen gradually over a few weeks or even a month or more, or they can happen suddenly.

As a result, even though they indicate that you are moving forward, they are not always reliable indicators of when labor actually began. Even if you are very dilated, it may take weeks before you give birth. Or, your cervix might be closed and high during an examination one morning but open and prepared for action — and labor — by noon.

Massage the perineum

Perineal massage is a bit awkward, but it may help to gently stretch your perineum, the region of skin between your vagina and rectum, which in turn can lessen the "stinging" that happens when a baby's head crowns during childbirth. Additionally, it might prevent tearing and an episiotomy for you.

It's best to avoid DIYing it the first time if you want to give it a try. Find a pelvic floor therapist who can demonstrate the proper technique for you. (Word of advice: Be kind.) Once you've mastered your craft, you can either carry on as you are or have your practitioner take over during labor.

37th week of pregnancy symptoms

Modifications in fetal activity
Acid reflux or indigestion
gruesome show
dilated veins
Pelvic pain
Leg twitches
Stretch stains
breast adjustments
Obstetrical brain

Insomnia

This Week's Tips for Oversleeping
Normal weight gain is gradual.

You're not gaining the pound per week you've come to anticipate in the third trimester. That's alright. It's possible that you didn't gain any weight at all last month.

Take longer between meals.

Experiencing more swelling than ever? Your digestion is slowed down by the pregnancy hormone progesterone, which results in bloating and cramping.

Eat your meals slowly as one strategy for preventing bloat. You swallow more than just food when you consume your lunch in less than five minutes. You also swallow a lot of air, which eventually forms gas bubbles in your stomach.

Purchase a fitness ball.

Want to stay active during your late pregnancy? Step up your game! You can safely and effectively strengthen your core muscles while pregnant by using an exercise ball. Additionally, in the not-too-distant future, it can offer much-needed physical relief and relaxation during pregnancy and labor.

Cast the stomach.

Belly casts have a long history and were once used to celebrate the miracle of birth. Making these DIY plaster replicas is simple and enjoyable. Sit back and watch as your chosen one(s) applies wet plaster strips to your belly (it usually dries within 15 minutes).

WEEK 38

EXPLORE WEEK38 0f PREGNANCY

Month 9 of pregnancy is roughly halfway through at 38 weeks.

Your baby is getting ready to make her entrance into the world and her lungs are getting stronger.

It might happen sooner than you anticipate, especially if you have a mucus plug or bloody period as a warning.

How much does my baby weigh at 38 weeks?

With an approximate weight of 7 pounds and an approximate length of 20 inches, your little one is no longer quite so tiny. There are only two — at most four — more weeks until your baby is born!

All systems are essentially set at 38 weeks of pregnancy! She is getting ready in a big way as well and is continuing to shed vernix and lanugo as you get ready for the arrival of the baby.

Consider these final weeks as a practice run for life with your newborn while you wait for your baby to arrive. Lack of sleep, mild anxiety, and leaking breasts.

Huh? Breast leaks? True, it is true: Colostrum, a thin, yellowish liquid that serves as the precursor to breast milk, often begins to leak from pregnant women during the third trimester.

It contains more protein, less fat and sugar, and is better for the baby's digestive system than the later-delivered milk because it is full of antibodies that protect your newborn. Consider nursing pads in your bra to protect your clothing if you are leaking colostrum, and get used to it since this is just a preview of what's to come.

However, not all women go through it. If not, don't worry; if you intend to breastfeed, your breasts are still producing colostrum for your child when the time comes.

Maternity Symptoms Week 3

increased urination
snot plug
gruesome show
Diarrhea
belly itch

Edema (swelling in feet and ankles) (swelling in feet and ankles)
Insomnia
nesting behavior
breast leakage
Braxton contractions of Hicks

Advice for This Week

Prepare meals for new mothers

Have you imagined yourself as a domestic goddess after giving birth who prepared fancy meals during the postpartum period? Dream away. In the initial weeks or even months following delivery, cooking won't even cross your mind or be on your to-do list.

Plan ahead to avoid having cereal for dinner every night. Stock your freezer right away with individually packaged, straightforward heat-and-serve options so you can quickly get food on the table. Label precisely so that you won't end up with UFOs (unidentified frozen objects).

The freezer is a good place for hearty soups, stews, casseroles, and mini meatloaves. Or, if you enjoy baking, keep a few trays of bran muffins in reserve; you'll need them. If you haven't already, the time is now to locate some excellent places to get takeout.

Check your bag once more

Verify that everything you packed in your hospital bag still fits you. Your prenatal pajamas may now be too snug. Do you still enjoy the snacks you brought?

Take a walk

Walking is one of the best exercises during pregnancy because it is easy on your knees and ankles.

There is yet another advantage to walking, although at this point it might be more accurate to refer to it as "waddling." Your baby's head may enter your pelvis more easily while you're walking—or waddling—giving you an advantage over labor.

Some people claim that a long walk can actually start labor contractions, speaking of labor. So as you approach or pass your due date, keep your sneaks close at hand.

Don loose, breathable clothing.

these days, perpetually damp? Once more, those hormones are in play. You may perspire like a linebacker as a result of their effects, as well as increased metabolism and blood flow to the skin during pregnancy.

Wear airy, loose-fitting clothing, consume plenty of water, open some windows, or turn the air conditioning up to keep cool. A light dusting of talc-free powder can also help absorb some moisture and prevent heat rash, which could develop under all that sweat. Perform squat drills.

Have you ever heard of women in the past giving birth on the ground wherever they happened to be? It seems there is some truth to it after all: Because squatting widens the pelvic opening and allows more space for the baby to descend, it actually quickens the labor process.

Don't worry; this doesn't mean that you should go to the fields the moment your contractions begin. To be a stronger squatter when the time comes—in the hospital or birthing center, that is—start incorporating squats into your exercise regimen now.

Try some labor-intensive foods

By the time your due date approaches, you're probably ready to try anything to have that million-dollar prize (your baby) sooner.

Unfortunately, there is no magic food that will induce labor, at least not according to medical science.

Can't hurt, might help foods include things like eggplant, balsamic vinegar, and anything spicy. There is no evidence that any of these will make you work harder, but many people swear by them.

There is no harm in trying if your stomach can handle the heat (late-pregnancy heartburn can be deadly!), as long as the allegedly magical foods don't replace healthy food options in your diet.

EXPLORE WEEK39 0f PREGNANCY

Congratulations are due: Now that month 9 is coming to an end, your baby is regarded as full-term!

Although your adorable baby is unaware that you are expecting him any moment, you can be sure that he has most likely reached his birth weight (or very close to it!) and will emerge when he is ready.

You should be on the lookout for labor symptoms at 39 weeks, and if it hasn't been done already, pack your hospital bag.

How much does my baby weigh at 39 weeks?

You are currently 39 weeks pregnant, which is when a baby is considered to be full-term. At this point, your baby is between 7 and 8 pounds and 19 and 21 inches long.

These measurements won't change much going forward, but his brain will continue to grow at an incredible rate for the next three years, changes you'll be able to see firsthand as your child's repertoire of skills grows almost daily.

symptoms of labor

You should be on the lookout for labor symptoms given that you can give birth at any time.

Labor is probably just a day or two away once you've seen bloody show, but don't try to set your watch to it since it's not a set schedule. Make sure your bag is packed, though!

Getting ready for a C-section

Even if delivery occurs via C-section, many hospitals and birthing facilities are becoming more considerate of expectant mothers' wishes to be awake, comfortable, and surrounded by loved ones both during and after delivery.

These days, the majority of places will try to meet as many of your requests as possible in a non-emergency situation, regardless of whether you have a scheduled C-section or induction or are already in labor.

To see your baby emerge, ask if you can use a mirror or clear screen.

Additionally, you might be able to breastfeed in the recovery room, have your partner cut the cord, and have your hands free to hold your newborn after birth. It won't harm you to ask for what you want at this particular moment.

39th week of pregnancy symptoms

Braxton contractions of Hicks

The fetal activity changing

Acid reflux or indigestion

gruesome show

mucus plug loss

breaking water

Diarrhea

Hemorrhoids

Pelvic pain

Tips for Backaches This Week

Your water has it a leak?

Unsure if your water has yet broken? It's likely urine, not amniotic fluid, which has no odor, if you awaken in a pool of ammonia-smelling fluid after the flow has stopped.

You won't be able to stop the leak as easily as you would if you were going to the bathroom if your water breaks.

Try a facial at home.

Treat yourself to a facial mask at home if your skin needs a boost or if you're just passing the time while you wait for your baby to arrive.

One quick trick is to add a few essential ingredients to a cup of plain yogurt based on your skin type: avocado and honey for dry skin, strawberries and lemon juice for oily skin.

Steam your face for five minutes before applying, and then leave the mixture on for 20 minutes for the best results.

You won't be able to stop the leak as easily as you would if you were going to the bathroom if your water breaks.

If you want a quick exfoliating scrub, combine some oatmeal with warm water to make a paste, then apply the mixture to your skin. After rinsing, your skin will be as smooth as the bottom of your unborn child.

Eating during labor Studies have shown that women who are given the option to eat during labor experience shorter labors, sometimes by as much as 16 minutes.

After all, labor is as laborious as its name implies, and labor demands fuel. It can be challenging to muster the energy for those final pushes when you're working on empty.

You won't be able to stop the leak as easily as you would if you were going to the bathroom if your water breaks.

Think small and try to stick to your healthcare team's recommendations if your practitioner gives the okay to eat. In general, small snacks and liquids can keep you hydrated and energized. Remain with broth, plain pasta, toast with jam, ice pops, sorbet, applesauce, or Jell-O.

Go to sleep

Breathe easily! Your body is exerting extra effort to support the fully developed baby inside of you. When you can, take a nap, and delegate chores to others.

The term "lightning crotch" exists.

Do your legs experience pains that radiate from your genital area? The "lightning crotch," which may be brought on by your baby pressing against the pelvic nerves, is nothing to be concerned about.

The good news is that it's neither risky nor an indication that something is wrong.

breech child? Try it.

Many nurse-midwives advise specific exercises you can perform to help turn your breech baby head-down, which is the best birthing exit strategy.

Try pelvic tilts or bending over while kneeling with your knees hip-width apart so that your breasts almost touch the floor. Three times a day, repeat. Good fortune!

Expect fetal electronic monitoring

Most likely, your baby will have a smooth birth because she or he is eager to meet the world. But some babies don't like the tight squeeze through the pelvis after spending the previous nine months floating peacefully inside your uterus.

You'll probably be connected to an electronic fetal monitor so your doctors can continue to watch how your baby is handling labor if there is a change in your baby's heart rate, such as a rapid acceleration or a slowed-down movement.

WEEK 40

EXPLORE WEEK40 0f PREGNANCY

You are technically still in month 9 of pregnancy even though you are 40 weeks pregnant (even if it feels like longer).

Your child has all of the necessary organs and reflexes to function normally outside of the womb.

If your due date has passed, you're in good company: A third of pregnancies will reach 41 weeks!

after the due date?

You're not alone if baby hasn't arrived this week: About 30% of pregnancies continue past the 40-week point.

How much does my baby weigh at 40 weeks?

Your baby's current weight and size are most likely between 6 and 9 pounds and 19 and 22 inches, although many perfectly healthy babies are born smaller or larger.

You've reached the official end of your pregnancy when you're 40 weeks along. For the first six months of her life, you or the placenta are still giving her the antibodies she needs to fight off infections.

However, if you intend to breastfeed, your milk will offer more immune-boosting antibodies, particularly colostrum, a thin, yellowish precursor to breast milk that is incredibly rich in antibodies and feeds your baby for the first few days after delivery.

Your baby might enjoy being swaddled.

Your child may move her arms and legs a little, but she is still curled up in the fetal position, as you'll see. That's because it'll take your baby some time to realize she has room to spread out after nine months in such confined spaces.

It's also a comforting position to be in because it's the only one she's really known. It also resembles your uterus, which is why many newborns (though not all!) enjoy being swaddled.

Will you continue to the due date?

When will your body be able to deliver this baby on its own? Even though your due date is written in pen on your doctor's chart and highlighted in red on your calendar, that doesn't mean Mother Nature is aware of the situation.

Nobody knows when your pregnancy will end because about 30% of all pregnancies last longer than 40 weeks. Fortunately, your doctor won't let it go any longer than 41 weeks.

When your water will break, if at all

Your water breaking, or the rupture of the amniotic sac that has been surrounding your baby for the past nine months, is one circumstance that is not always guaranteed before the start of labor.

You've probably already missed a few hours of sleep worrying about the time and location. You've probably heard or seen horror stories about how someone's water broke at an awkward — no, make that humiliating — time and place, like in the middle of a busy sidewalk during lunch or at a packed public place.

. However, your reality show will probably differ slightly from mine.

First of all, less than 15% of women experience a rupture of the membranes prior to the start of labor, and secondly, if your water does break in public, it's more likely to come as a slow leak, trickle, or small gush rather than a torrential tidal wave.

If your water breaks before your contractions have begun, one thing is for certain: Within 24 hours, labor will likely start in earnest. Either that, or within 24 hours, your doctor will start it for you.

What symptoms point to an amniotic sac rupture? Amniotic fluid typically has no color and no smell. If you observe a yellowish-colored fluid and if it leaks urine and smells like ammonia, you probably are. Another test: Squeezing your pelvic muscles might help you try to stop the fluid from flowing (Kegel exercises). Urine will flow if the flow stops. If not, the substance is amniotic fluid.

Call your practitioner as soon as your water breaks if the fluid is green or brown. It might imply that your unborn child had meconium in utero, which is a bowel movement.

Labor phobias

Many women share the unfounded worry that they won't be able to give birth to their child. It does seem unlikely that something so large—a 6- or 7-plus-pound watermelon—could fit through such a small opening, but most of the time it does.

The majority of newborns are fairly well matched to their mothers' sizes because Mother Nature knows what to do.

Your vagina is also aware of what to do because it miraculously tightens up again after experiencing significant stretching during childbirth. By performing your Kegels consistently both before and after delivery, you can speed up that process. Even your infant knows how to handle the situation by molding that still-pliable head to fit through the small opening. Don't worry, then!

40th week of pregnancy symptoms

Braxton contractions of Hicks
Modifications in fetal activity
cervical effacement or dilation
Diarrhea
Pelvic pain
Leg twitches
Insomnia
nesting behaviour

Advice for This Week
Inquire about causing labor.

Ask your doctor when, why, and how you might be put under induction. It is typically not advised to induce labor before week 39 of pregnancy, unless there are health or medical reasons to do so. Around week 41, many doctors start inducing.

Have a backup strategy in case of a home birth

Low-risk pregnancies can be safely delivered at home, but if you need to be induced or your baby requires more medical attention, you might need to give birth in a hospital.

If you decide to give birth at home, discuss with your healthcare provider when this might be necessary and how the delivery will proceed from there.

safely shaving

Feeling a bit more furry than usual these days? Due to the fact that A) your balance may be off and B) you probably can't see past your belly, shave those legs carefully and liberally with nick-protecting shaving gel. To reduce your risk of drawing blood, use a brand-new razor.

Shaving in the shower is a no-no, as a mistake there could have serious repercussions.

Consider hydrotherapy

Hydrotherapy is a complementary or alternative pain reliever that's used to treat pregnancy aches and pains and can also be helpful during labor, much like hypnobirthing and massage.

You might want to take a warm bath or shower, or get warm or cold compresses applied to your pelvis or lower back when the contractions start. Alternately, you could decide to give birth in a bathtub and allow the warm water to ease your contractions.

But as soon as it's time to start pushing, you should get out of the bath. Babies born underwater are susceptible to a number of potentially life-threatening complications.

Make a quick workout.

Lacking the stamina for a lengthy sweat session? Make a quick workout.

Turn slowly from side to side while allowing your arms to swing freely.

You can also clench your butt and let go after counting to two. To pass the time and tone your muscles, try performing 15 or 20 arm swings and butt clenches.

When the contractions start, try to relax.

Of course you're anxious and excited as can be, but you should make an effort to relax as much as you can during the early stages of labor because you'll need to conserve your energy for when things get tough.

Try your best to get some sleep if it's late at night because you won't be able to once your contractions start to become more frequent. During the day, keep yourself occupied.

Try going for a walk; it might even make the contractions stronger. Simply stay close to home and never leave the house without a phone.

At this point, don't worry about obsessively timing your contractions; if you do, you might end up frustrated. However, you should periodically check to see if they're getting closer together. When the first stage of labor is over and the second one starts, the majority of people go to the hospital.

Intentionally left blank

WEEK 41

EXPLORE WEEK41 0f PREGNANCY

Be prepared: You are 41 weeks along and due soon (and your original due date may well have been a little off).

The benefit? Your child will be a little more alert and have longer fingernails when they are born!

Keep an eye out for contractions or other signs that labor is about to start even though you've probably already discussed labor induction with your practitioner.

How much do I weigh at 41 weeks?

Your baby is roughly the size of a pumpkin and measures between 19 and 22 inches at 41 weeks.

Baby due soon?

According to the statistics, it appears that your baby chose the quite common option of a late checkout. Less than 5% of infants are actually born on their due dates, and 10% decide to overstay their welcome at Hotel Uterus.

Also keep in mind that an overdue baby is frequently not actually overdue; rather, the due date was mistaken. That's alright; at 41 weeks along, there is still work to be done.

Get set and go!

Your body is currently in the best possible condition for giving birth. Although your doctor has likely discussed labor induction with you by the time you are 41 weeks pregnant, it doesn't necessarily follow that you won't experience spontaneous labor; some infants simply require more time. But here's the concern you keep having: Will you be able to recognize labor when you feel it?

contractions of labor

You will likely be aware of it. But just in case, here is a brief introduction. Just before labor starts, your water may break (or it may not), and you might notice pink or red mucus, also known as bloody show.

Then you'll experience labor contractions, which are rhythmic waves of your uterus' hardening and softening. For some women, these waves can start suddenly and quickly, while for others, they may come on gradually and steadily. They often, but not always, begin farther apart and then gradually get closer together.

Menstrual cramps or a low backache may be how you feel during your first real contractions. The pain frequently starts in your back and spreads to your front. However, just as no two pregnancies are alike, neither are any two labors. Although there are some textbook labors, a surprising number of them break the rules.

Call your practitioner and describe the contractions if you feel them but are unsure if they are the real thing. Your doctor or midwife should be able to determine whether you are in labor based on the sound of your voice and a thorough description of your symptoms.

Week 41 of pregnancy symptoms

Fetal activity changes More frequent urination

gruesome show

cervical effacement or dilation

Diarrhea

Hemorrhoids

Pelvic pain

Overdue Advice for You This Week: Nesting Instinct Don't worry

Even though you've gone over 40 weeks, you're not necessarily past due. In reality, it's thought that in 70% of post-term pregnancies, the due date and/or conception date were mistaken, leading to the pregnancy.

You may reduce your weight.

If your pregnancy is coming to an end, your weight gain is also coming to an end. The numbers on the scale may not change at 41 weeks, or they may even be declining.

Your body slows down (or comes to a standstill) to prepare for labor; this is a sign that everything is preparing for the major event. When your body's baby-making factory stops, it is actively ridding itself of the fluid it won't need, which results in a decrease in amniotic fluid and an increase in urine (and possibly poop).

Additionally, you may be losing weight as a result of increased sweating, which will become a habit in the weeks following delivery. Your body will increase sweat production during the first postpartum week in particular to remove all the fluid that has accumulated over the previous nine months.

Learn what to anticipate during labor.

If you need anything to stay at ease and comfortable, such as a back rub, ice chips, or a washcloth to cool your face, don't be afraid to ask your coach for it. If this is your first time, keep in mind that your partner or coach may find it challenging to anticipate your needs.

If you're using breathing exercises, you'll begin them when your contractions become too intense for you to talk through them. Try to shift positions during contractions. The hospital's staff will be there to time your contractions and keep an eye on the baby's development.

If you receive an epidural, you may also be fitted with a continuous fetal monitor and an IV to keep your fluid levels stable after it is administered. You might not be able to move your legs very much unless you have a walking epidural, but if you can, try to switch positions frequently.

Reduce back pain while sleeping

An aching back can be greatly relieved by a firm mattress. Try putting a board under your side of the bed for the remainder of your pregnancy if yours is on the softer side.

You can also get more comfortable at night by using a body pillow that is at least 5 feet long, which can take the pain out of some sleeping positions.

Enjoy yourself while you wait.

Now that your due date has passed, you're probably eager to get going. Be kind to yourself, though. Rest and unwind as much as you can. If you can, go outside for some fresh air and exercise each day. However, don't overdo it or worry too much.

Everything will be fine as long as you keep in close contact with your doctor and have a plan in place in case your baby needs a little prod to venture out into the world. You'll soon be nostalgically remembering your days of freedom. Make the most of your "me time" right away.

www.ingramcontent.com/pod-product-compliance
Lightning Source LLC
Chambersburg PA
CBHW070511160726
48003CB00004B/1525